MW01032620

"GETTING OUT OF THE BOX"

IS SOMETHING LIKE ESCAPING A PRISON, WHICH ONE CANNOT REALLY ACHIEVE UNLESS ONE LEARNS A GREAT DEAL ABOUT THE NATURE OF THE PRISON ITSELF.

Most reality-box constructions omit mention of how awesome and wonderful the individual and collective consciousness of our species actually is. Even so, this magical aspect of ourselves can be retrieved from the many wreckages brought about via conflicting reality-box endeavors.

In this lucid and absorbing work, Ingo Swann opens up the continuing story about the fuller extent of human consciousness...

Ingo Swann (1933-2013) was an American artist and exceptionally successful subject in parapsychology experiments. As a child he spontaneously had numerous paranormal experiences, mostly of the OBE type, the future study of which became a major passion as he matured. In 1970, he began acting as a parapsychology test subject in tightly controlled laboratory settings with numerous scientific researchers. Because of the success of most of these thousands of test trials, major media worldwide often referred to him as "the scientific psychic."

His subsequent research on behalf of American intelligence interests, including that of the CIA, won him top PSI-spy status.

His involvement in government research projects required the discovery of innovative approaches toward the actual realizing of subtle human energies. He viewed PSI powers as only parts of the larger spectrum of human sensing systems and was internationally known as an advocate and researcher of the exceptional powers of the human mind.

To learn more about Ingo, his work, art, and other books, please visit: **www.ingoswann.com.**

REALITY BOXES

AND OTHER BLACK HOLES
IN HUMAN CONSCIOUSNESS

A BIOMIND SUPERPOWERS BOOK
PUBLISHED BY

Swann-Ryder Productions, LLC
www.ingoswann.com

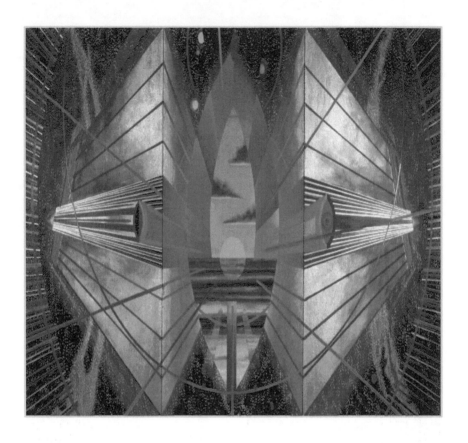

Copyright © 2003 by Ingo Swann; Copyright © 2015 by Murleen S.
Ryder; Copyright © 2017 by Swann-Ryder Productions, LLC.

All rights reserved.
No part of this book may be used or reproduced in any manner
whatsoever without written permission.
For more information address: www.ingoswann.com.

Previously published in trade paperback by Ingo Swann Books
and digitally by Crossroad Press.

First edition BioMind Superpowers Books.

Cover art: *Existence* by Ingo Swann © Swann-Ryder Productions, LLC.

Cube graphic created by Pixabay.

ISBN-13: 978-1-949214-84-0

REALITY
BOXES

INGO SWANN

WHAT IS THE ACTUAL EXTENT OF HUMAN CONSCIOUSNESS?

DURING THE TWENTIETH century, various efforts were undertaken to study consciousness, but only from within this or that theory or model.

In keeping with these efforts, one might think that it was important to find out and document what, on a broad scale, individuals actually experience via consciousness independently of the guidelines of the theories or models utilized to study it.

Yet, nothing like this ever took place. Many of the theories and models were intolerant of aspects of consciousness that did not fit into them, and many aspects were, in the first place, taboo, pre-rejected as impossible, and even alien and unfamiliar within the guidelines.

The problematical outcome of all this is that while some few aspects of consciousness may have been better described and understood, what can be thought of as the entire scope, extent, or spectrum of human consciousness remains unidentified – except as various aspects of that spectrum are experienced by individuals.

The problem here does not involve the fuller extent of consciousness itself as something everyone is innately born with, but how consciousness is treated within various socio-environmental situations.

Indeed, it is generally acknowledged today that all sociological structures do (and have in the past) treat consciousness and its spectrum in radically different ways.

But this directly implies that the fuller spectrum of

human consciousness is always in some sort of bondage within this or that sociological perspective, each of which establishes parameters of tolerance and intolerance with respect to various aspects of the whole of human consciousness as it exists throughout our species.

This helps shed light on something that otherwise remains very puzzling: why there is a very large and very traditional lack of interest in what INDIVIDUALS actually experience of consciousness.

After all, if consciousness IS to be studied, then it seems logical to impartially ascertain, as broadly as possible, what the manifold carriers of it actually experience – which is EVERYONE born of our species.

As it is, however, the consciousness of all individuals who are encapsulated within the typical sociological structure is supposed to conform to ideas of it that are socially determined.

This means that different kinds of sociological ambience have held sway over how consciousness is supposed to function, and thus what individuals might experience in contrast to that ambience has consistently been of little interest.

Now, at the beginning of the twenty-first century it is newly being perceived, even if only roughly so, that there is MORE to human consciousness overall than can neatly be fitted into past ideas of it.

One reason is that the cultures and social orders of the world are in closer proximity to one and another than they have ever been – principally because they find themselves closely linked via the global Internet and other forms of swift intercommunication.

Because of this, it is being seen more than ever that cultures and social orders have had different local realities, which is to say, have had idea-formats that have inspired the construction, in consciousness, of different kinds of reality "boxes." Thus, it is slowly being understood that different kinds of reality boxes can be set up in human consciousness, which then serve to limit concepts of consciousness to the various idea-formats of them.

So, it can be wondered if reality boxes are all there is to human consciousness per se, and if not, then what else does the rest of it consist of. The only real clue has to do with what individuals experience outside of given reality boxes – which is a great deal, indeed.

The central purpose of this book is to add to already on-going inquiry with respect to the importance of what human individuals experience of or via consciousness, and which experiencing is building a bigger picture of the fuller extent of human consciousness itself.

CONSCIOUSNESS

IS

AND IT IS BIGGER
THAN YOU THINK

This book is dedicated to the
Motherboard of human
consciousness and to those
who have awareness of it.

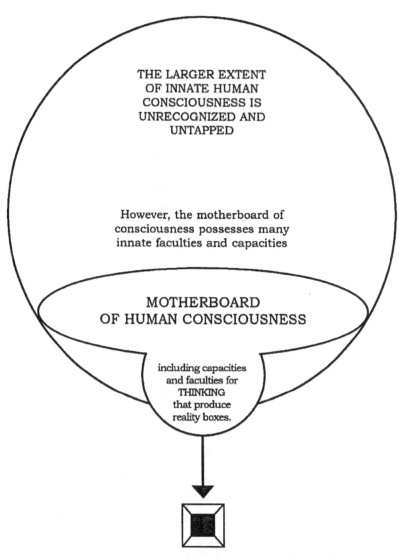

THE LARGER EXTENT
OF INNATE HUMAN
CONSCIOUSNESS IS
UNRECOGNIZED AND
UNTAPPED

However, the motherboard of
consciousness possesses many
innate faculties and capacities

MOTHERBOARD
OF HUMAN CONSCIOUSNESS

including capacities
and faculties for
THINKING
that produce
reality boxes.

Boxed realities are limited versions of reality achieved by
avoiding or rejecting realities that do not accord with the limited
version. Boxed realities are usually thought of as complete in
themselves, and so there is no awareness or recognition of
knowledge that is absent or missing in them.
What IS missing or absent in boxed realities is usually more
significant than whatever is present in them.

Contents

I don't see the logic of rejecting data just because they seem incredible.

Astronomer Sir Fred Hoyle (1915-2001)

Introduction

A BEGINNING STIMULUS for this volume developed shortly after 1969 when the American intelligence agencies became aware that the Soviet Union, its KGB, and its military were officially conducting major secret research into the paranormal.

This came as something of a shock to the American intelligence agencies that had long considered the paranormal as little more than a giggle factor. However, when the actual scope of the Soviet research was confirmed as extensive, alarm bells began going off throughout high government levels and the giggle factor quickly began to undergo reassessment.

An important mandate of the intelligence services is to study the threat potential of any development anywhere. So the Soviet research was soon perceived as such a threat since it might ultimately include advanced and efficient forms of mind-reading or invasive forms of psychic mind-control and influencing over distances.

One of the first situations that needed to be addressed was how to convert what was just yesterday an ignored giggle factor into a serious, in-depth study of something that tomorrow might have serious ramifications.

The initial responses with respect to this changeover were somewhat hysterical and comical, accompanied, however, by surges of serious interest in erecting psychic shields so that minds could not be penetrated.

Soon, however, it was realized that the conventional intelligence services were out of their depth, so, by the middle of 1972, it was decided to form a government-sponsored research project to help assess the threat, and to house it at Stanford Research Institute (SRI) in California.

At that time, SRI was, after the Rand Corporation, the second largest think tank in the United States, and also one of the major research arms of the Pentagon and other governmental agencies. This development meant that the governments of the two leading superpowers of the world were involving themselves in, of all things, psychic research.

News of THIS development leaked into the ever-excitable media always lusting for fabulous stories, and so the public was extensively informed that a psychic war was already underway, and that a psychic gap unfavorable to all Americans had been discovered.

By a series of chance events, it transpired in 1972 that this author was invited to be a part of the new project at SRI that endured for the following rather exciting, but often bumpy sixteen years.

At the beginning of the project, it became apparent that the personnel of the government sponsors knew very little about the paranormal. As a result, the SRI project was to provide the government sponsors with a series of bigger-picture informative background papers about it.

One of these papers dealt with the historical sociological treatment of the paranormal, PSI, ESP, and so forth, with special emphasis of such treatment during the nineteenth and twentieth centuries.

This particular paper, never undertaken anywhere before, required the efforts of eight research individuals and some eighteen months to prepare.

When completed, it elegantly showed, with numerous graphs and charts, that psychic gaps do exist, essentially because of societal taboo-like resistance to any development of psychic faculties and other aspects of the paranormal.

It also showed that paranormal phenomena were conceptualized, during the late 1800s and early 1900s, not as inherent aspects of consciousness itself, but as unusual, separate, and specific products of (the) mind.

This led to intellectual attempts to isolate and methodologically categorize each of the products, and then to study their workings via theories as to how each might independently function.

It seemed a logical approach at first. But by the late 1960s it had become increasingly difficult to distinguish between the mental workings of, say, telepathy, clairvoyance, out-of-body experience, etc.

This meant that the mental workings of (the) mind did not take place in accordance with the intellectual categories earlier envisioned.

However, an unexpected benefit of the paper revealed that paranormal elements continuously emerge time and again throughout history on a scope much larger than was generally understood, but only to be re-submerged, by somewhat disgusting means, beneath conventional sociological overviews antagonistic to paranormal elements.

It was this early 1970s paper that provided the basic stimuli for the contents of this present volume, but which, for several reasons, goes far beyond the limited contexts available back then.

For example, when the original paper was produced, we were confined within the limitations of the terminology then available.

The paranormal could only be referred to as such, or by some variant of it, such as PSI, psychic, parapsychology, ESP, or powers of mind, etc., all of these being understood as paranormal in character.

As it has turned out by now, however, the term paranormal, along with its variants, is in eclipse and out of fashion, having been replaced by the phrase Exceptional Human Experiencing.

So, with the exception of powers of mind (which still remains relevant), it will no longer be utilized in the text ahead except in the case of a past historical context.

The central focus of the 1970s paper was on sociological objections to the paranormal as it was then conceptualized. In this volume, the central focus and emphasis is on exceptional human experiencing itself, on its magnitude, and on some of its very many variants.

Back in the 1970s, the concept of mindsets represented the only understood way of discussing formed attitudes and preconceptions vested in certain limited parameters.

Therefore, the only way to discuss the sociological objections was to associate them with mindsets that were opposed, for one
reason or another, to any opening up of positive-oriented research into any aspect of the paranormal.

As it has also turned out, the concept of mindsets has been almost entirely replaced by the concept of reality boxes. This is a favorable conceptual advance in that mindsets seem to refer to thinking patterns that have become trained or conditioned one way or another, whereas reality boxes seem more to relate to consciousness itself.

Admittedly, this may be a subtle distinction between mind and consciousness, but it can be thought that mind might not exist without consciousness, and if so, the latter is greater than the former.

In the early 1970s, the concept of consciousness had not yet acquired the luminosity it began to achieve in the early 1980s.

The term was in use, of course. But it was generally understood as referring only to the awake state, while all else such as the subconscious, unconscious, non-conscious, and super-consciousness were not exactly thought of as expandable elements of consciousness itself.

In fact, the concept of the paranormal seems largely to have been brought into usage to distinguish between what was thought of as the average dimensions of normal awake consciousness and variations of consciousness awareness that did not fit into or could be explained within the average.

During the 1980s, the crass distinctions between awake consciousness and OTHER forms of consciousness began to break down.

Several reasons for this can be detected. But a principal one was that numerous broad polls in the United States were taken during that decade asking individuals what they experienced of the paranormal.

Almost a century earlier in the 1890s, a similar kind of "international" census had been taken in England and Europe, the results of which were reported in English by Edmund Parish under the title of HALLUCINATIONS AND ILLUSIONS: A STUDY OF THE FALLACIES OF PERCEPTION (1897).

The title of this report reveals the prevailing attitudes of the time, in that the Victorians of the era were not all that forthcoming about experiencing "hallucinations."

In any event, after admittedly sorting and tossing out many responses as evidence only of mental derangement, Parish indicated that only 5 to 10 percent of individuals interviewed might have possibly experienced something of strange but real substance.

Eighty years later, however, the American polls resulted in

radically higher percentages. In some categories, many of the polls indicated that as many as 75 percent of those interviewed had consciously experienced some form of paranormal consciousness.

Since any statistic above 50 percent can be thought of as a majority, and hence qualify as normal, the concept of the paranormal began to become normalized, after which the term also became useless, and was ultimately replaced during the 1990s by the concept of exceptional human experiencing.

The foregoing has been a rather longish way to synopsize a lot of intriguing history, but it serves to highlight a very important distinction.

This has to do with the question of what the consciousness of humans can and does experience VERSUS what they are supposed only to experience within the limits of this or that sociological norm.

One can flop around a lot in trying to figure out how that question might begin to be answered. But certainly, there is a fundamental launch pad that is entirely relevant.

Everyone is born with innate consciousness set and ready to go

If THIS is accepted, then all subsequent questions seem to pivot on what happens to innate consciousness AFTER one is born with it.

NOTE: In the text ahead, many words and terms relevant to consciousness per se are defined and examined, and shifts in their historical meanings are traced. Unless otherwise noted, I have depended on the Oxford Dictionary of the English Language and Webster's Seventh New Collegiate Dictionary (1967). Both of these are replete with precise definitions and explanatory information that has often become garbled or gone missing in subsequent dictionaries.

CONSCIOUSNESS OF OUR POWERS AUGMENTS THEM.
Marquis de Vauvenarques (1715-1747)

PART ONE

OBSERVATIONS ABOUT HUMAN CONSCIOUSNESS

Chapter One

ARE WE OVER-ENDOWED WITH RESPECT TO MERE SURVIVAL ON EARTH?

1

THE DISCUSSIONS presented in this book are based on two important factors, both of which are largely ignored.

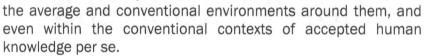

First, many individuals feel they are MORE than what they have become within the average and conventional environments around them, and even within the conventional contexts of accepted human knowledge per se.

Second, there exists abundant research that can altogether be referred to as powers of human consciousness. The larger sum of this research ultimately suggests that the human species is equipped with capacities that are neither used nor nurtured, but which anyway survive through the generations in some kind of latent form.

The existence of such capacities is demonstrated in all cultures when individuals chance to experience what today is referred to as products of altered states of consciousness.

The capacities of insight and intuition are probably the best known of these altered states. But several statistical polls and studies undertaken during the last thirty years reveal that the faculties of clairvoyance, telepathy, and precognition are also frequently experienced.

However, these particular faculties are but the tip of the greater totality of human consciousness potentials, and as will be discussed throughout the sections ahead, the brief enumeration just above can be extended by hundreds of such potentials.

2

It is not the purpose of the considerations presented in this book to argue on behalf of the real existence of these capacities.

Many have already done so over the last hundred and fifty years or more. And, for example, if the combined sum of modern brain-mind, consciousness, and parapsychology research is given the merit deserved, then the existence of such capacities cannot really be discounted.

It is also not the purpose to present discussions only in the contexts of parapsychology and consciousness research, even though those contexts have undeniable importance. Rather, the considerations presented have a two-fold purpose in terms of human sociology.

The first part of this purpose is to point up that our species and its individuals are apparently over-endowed with capacities and faculties that are far in excess of what is needed to live in the sociological ways of our average and conventional social structures.

Indeed, it can be established that most social structures do not need too much extensive consciousness in order to function as they do, and clearly do not need extraordinary manifestations of its larger extent and totality.

This can be explained in part by understanding and accepting the historical fact that almost all past cultures, however seen as great, otherwise, were fundamentally based on massive broadband slavery, serfdom, and various other under-classes whose principal function was to be in servitude to the upper overlords. Such was certainly the case, for example, in ancient Egyptian, Sumerian, Babylonian, Assyrian, Roman, Chinese, and most old Nordic cultures, etc.

Modern historians mention this of course, but then rather smoothly glide past any extended implications involved, one of which pertains to what happened to the innate consciousness of those in bondage and servitude.

Well, those in servitude did not need too much consciousness in order to perform their duties, and so it became important to ensure that the lower orders could not have democratic access to ways and means of enlarging their consciousness potentials.

This kind of thing is not yet absent. Thundering echoes of it persist in today's wage-slavery concepts and among the disenfranchised whose consciousness should remain compatible only with their lower-order status.

As will several times be exampled ahead, the best and most obvious way of ensuring this is to prevent knowledge of extended forms of consciousness from being studied and realized by anyone, including the upper classes, and which, as history documents, could use a little of their own extended forms.

The second part of the purpose is to point up that various extraordinary manifestations of consciousness appear spontaneously anyway within the larger scope of human experiencing, and have always done so throughout history and in all cultures.

It is because of the continuing historical frequency of such experiencing that human consciousness is certainly to be understood as being composed of much more than what is usually attributed to it.

3

There is an earlier precedent that is quite similar to the two points made above.

When the mapping of the human brain and its functions became possible not so long ago, many entirely respectable researchers offered up the idea that individuals used only about 10 percent of the probable potentials of their brains, although a genius might be using as much as 15 percent. What the rest of the brain was for was not really understood, and still isn't – except that it processes "information" at a truly astonishing velocity.

This situation led to some rather wobbly questions for which answers have not yet readily made an appearance.

One such question had to do with why human brains should be larger, so to speak, than the 10 percent normally utilized. It certainly does not suggest good biological economy of a structural organic nervous system in which everything has a vital role to play.

A possible hypothetical consideration is that whole human brain power is fundamentally meant to be utilized in the direct biological sense, but simply isn't in relation to human social structures on Earth in which too much brain power is not really needed.

The 10 percent analogy is not as interesting or significant as it once was sixty years ago, but only because advancing discovery has shifted emphasis away from it.

Even so, many today look around and have occasion to wonder what IS being used for brain power or consciousness, and how much of it – and it is thereby possible to conclude that not too much of it is underway.

The 10 percent analogy might thus be a little dated, but with a slight statistical shift it is applicable to the presumed totality of human consciousness. Indeed, on the cutting edge of research, it is deemed quite probable that individuals might have only 1 percent, or less, consciousness of all they might otherwise become conscious of, including a larger totality of themselves.

4

Before entering the sections ahead, it is absolutely necessary to point up the existence of a somewhat monumental stumbling block, but which is not given the attention it deserves.

This involves the distinction between (1) official research of human faculties and consciousness, and (2) the human experiencing of them at the individual level.

It is somewhat difficult to illuminate the distinction. But generally speaking, RESEARCH is laboriously conceptualized as "studious inquiry or examination, especially investigation or experimentation aimed at the discovery and interpretation of facts, revision of accepted theories or laws in the light of new facts, or practical application of such new or revised theories or laws."

The definition should be read several times, after which it might be possible for the perceptive eye to see that "theories or laws" constitute the backbone of research one way or another.

Now, theories or laws need not necessarily take into account what individuals actually experience, largely because doing so can be inconvenient to the theories and laws.

So, there is hardly any research field that does so. And if such a field really got going it would soon be seen that individuals collectively experience a great deal that cannot be fitted into known theories and laws – and have done so throughout history and on a planet-wide basis.

Thus, and as might be expected, some very wide gaps presently exist between research of human consciousness and what individuals actually experience.

5

For emphasis, in a certain sense, the Life-value of all individuals might be seen as more important than general theories or laws, if only because such theories and laws are often and usually "revised," etc.

But with respect to discovering general theories pertaining to brain-mind and consciousness research it can be understood that what can be considered in general is of interest, but that the particular is not – especially if the particular cannot be conveniently fitted into the general.

Thus, what particular individuals, or even groups of them, experience of brain-mind-consciousness activity is of little official general interest.

6

In the overall context of this book, the question thus emerges with respect to what DO individuals actually experience in terms of consciousness – and whether or not the experiencing fits into the general, the average, or the conventional.

Even a small safari into this question more than hints of something quite remarkable and magnificent – and of which each individual of our species is and always will be a reflection of, whether sociologically acknowledged or not.

Chapter Two

WHY DO WE FEEL THERE IS MORE TO US THAN WE, OR ANYONE, KNOWS ABOUT?

7

HERE AT the beginning of these discussions it might seem presumptuous of this author to suggest that there are, in the great rolling forward of knowledge, important issues that have escaped notice – issues that are almost never illuminated, and so most are hardly aware that they exist.

After all, we today live in a glut of information of all kinds. And so, it might be assumed that everything that is important must have already been identified.

This assumption can lead to another one – that there are no vacuums or black holes in knowledge as accumulated throughout the world so far.

Most realize that we depend on information that is accepted in official mainstream levels. Even so, many also *realize* that information unofficially exists outside those levels in occult, esoteric, and mystical traditions, etc.

Thus, if the official and unofficial information is put together, it is difficult to see how anything important has been missed.

8

As a way of getting into what is discussed in this volume, we need an example of something that has been missed, of something that has never been really brought to light, and so has never been given examination.

If throughout one's years one goes about the world, it is possible to encounter numerous people at all walks of life who, as already mentioned, feel that they are composed of more than what they have become.

The feeling might not be equally shared across the boards. For example, I asked a friend if he had such a feeling. He hesitated, but then responded: "Well, sometimes when I wake up in the morning. But by the end of the day . . ."

As a group, those who feel they are "more," may include discontents as well as the so-called "average" individual. But in this writer's experience, also included are highly successful individuals, and even those who have arrived at the peak of their professional achievements and historical importance.

It is not unusual to discover individuals who have achieved the top or end of their careers, especially when retiring, to ask: What, is THAT it? Is that all there is to life, to MY life, to MY existence?

And even the young can become aware that there is more to them than what their goals imply and what they are in process of doing and trying to achieve.

Many such individuals may not even be discontent with their lives as they are unfolding. Nevertheless, there can be, beyond their daily lives and activities, a brooding about the meanings of their existing in the first place.

It is not entirely possible, of course, to estimate how large this group may be. But it is NOT small.

9

Now, all of this might be thought of as a common situation within the overall Human Condition, because it is accepted that humans, as thinking organisms, often become worried about not only the meanings of their own existing, but also about the meaning of existence itself.

In the past, the major way this Human Condition situation was dealt with in broad societal terms was to see the Meaning of Existence as the larger issue, and then to turn it over to philosophical practitioners who were more or less entrusted with dissecting it.

This was certainly a long-term noble effort, and it should be respected as such. It produced an enormous volume of books and other published considerations, and if one undertakes to read through them, nuggets of information can be gleaned. So, it would be unfair to say that philosophical study constitutes a complete black hole within human knowledge.

But as is now generally recognized, however, the noble effort largely "failed" because rather steamy debates arose and were perpetuated among philosophical practitioners - and the issues surrounding the meaning of existence never did achieve too much clarity.

10

If one makes the rather long-term effort to study philosophical considerations about the meaning of existence, a particular realization might ultimately dawn.

This has to do with the place, so to speak, assigned to The Individual in philosophic considerations.

This place is practically non-existent in those considerations, and so it could be said that philosophic considerations are principally mounted only upon what philosophers think in general terms, rather than upon what people actually experience as individuals.

Thus, there appears to be what might be called "knowledge vacuums" within the contexts of philosophic considerations about the meaning of existence. After all, the meaning of existence can be important to all individuals, and many of them, if asked, might have some significant insights and intuitions about it.

Especially, for example, the elderly who have experienced not only the various pleasures and hardships of their lives, but also a great deal of life itself – but who are hardly ever asked to sum up the meanings of their existence, or of existence itself.

What happens instead is that the deducing of the meaning of existence seems to be left to philosophers who tend to theorize in general terms (and, it may as well be said, within the terms of their own reality boxes), after which many others attempt, in their own lives, to emulate the deductions.

Well, if the larger picture of the history of philosophy is studied, it becomes apparent that philosophers seldom see eye-to-eye about anything, especially about the meaning of human existence, and philosophy is, in observable fact, mostly characterized by internecine battles among them. Therefore, it is rather safe to say that neither the meanings, nor the mechanisms, of existence have been pinned down all that much.

This is not to say that nothing has ever come of philosophical considerations. As will be discussed ahead, there have indeed been many great philosophers who have managed to deposit "nuggets" of information, and which are "golden" simply because they make self-evident sense through the times and tides of the meaning of existence.

As a brief aside, consider the wide-ranging philosophical importance of the following maxim: "Real knowledge is to know the extent of one's ignorance."

Many have fresh, ongoing, and surprising occasions to grasp something along these lines, and so the sense it makes seems constantly reoccurring in the NOW.

However, this maxim was uttered, probably not for the first time, about 2,600 years ago, by the venerable Chinese sociologist and philosopher-sage Confucius (c.551-474? B.C.). (See ANALECTS OF CONFUCIUS, Vol. 2, Sec. 17).

It is worth pointing up (specifically for the contexts of this book) that Confucianism, in its early form, was entirely a system of ethical precepts for the proper management of society.

It envisaged man as essentially a social creature who is bound to his fellows by JEN, a Chinese concept for which there is no exact equivalent in English. It is usually rendered as "sympathy" or "human-heartedness," which, like empathy and intuition, need to be nurtured into experiencing in order to become effective.

In spite of the maxim's antiquity, it seems that most individuals principally operate on what they know, or think they do, to the degree that what they are ignorant of has little interest. This phenomenon is a chief characteristic of reality boxes – in some of which the four human elements of sympathy, human-heartedness, empathy, and intuitive linkage have not been nurtured all that much.

The four human elements of JEN are almost, if not entirely,

absent in the history of philosophic considerations specific to the cultural West. The sum result is that even though individuals might experience them, those elements have no official PLACE within the otherwise great philosophic networks of the West, inclusive of modern philosophies.

Yet these four elements are experienced all of the time, even if only at the (unofficial) individual level, especially that of intuitive linkage to, of all things, oneself, even if only at a subconscious level.

This self-intuitive-linkage has much to do with WHY so many individuals feel there is more to themselves and to their existing than can be accounted for by their daily lives.

The most basic answer is that individuals ARE more, and that there is indeed an uplifting more to them than fits within "existence" as they have been educated to understand it.

Based on significant evidence, it can be thought that if our species did NOT have uplifting powers of intuitive linkages, perhaps several kinds of them, then – well, just subtract sympathy, insight, and intuition from the total human package and consider where we would be without them. Down the tubes, as it were, and not too long after Day One of human existing.

Chapter Three

INDIVIDUAL HUMAN CONSCIOUSNESS

11

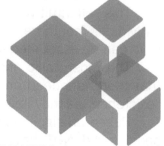

AN EXAMINATION of the numerous sources that seek to define the term CONSCIOUSNESS shows that whatever it really is, it is nevertheless hard to define.

Even so, the definitions of CONSCIOUSNESS so far seem to make sense, not because they DO make sense, but because each human individual is naturally endowed with consciousness as a species generic attribute.

It is therefore possible for everyone to recognize what is being talked about via the definitions because they ALREADY have what is being talked about even if only piecemeal – and would have it whether it was talked about or not.

Here, then, is the distinction of establishing what something IS, versus finding out what it can DO or DOES or is CAPABLE OF.

So, all things about consciousness that can be considered, it could be thought that what human consciousness is CAPABLE OF would have received some priority attention long ago.

Of course, that is not the case at all, and many manifestations and doings *of* consciousness are denied within the same efforts that seek to define it.

So, it seems that attempts to define what consciousness IS can go on. But what consciousness is capable of represents something of a black hole in collective human consciousness itself.

12

To elaborate more about this particular black hole, it is

necessary
to briefly review what consciousness IS, what it is thought to be.

HISTORICAL TIDBIT. The term CONSCIOUSNES came into English usage only in about 1630, and was accompanied by two principal definitions:

1) Internal knowledge or conviction, especially knowledge as to which one has the testimony within oneself; and
2) The state or fact of being mentally conscious or aware OF anything.

Up until the twentieth century, definitions for the term did not vary too much from those given above. But during that century, also the age of modern psychology, what CONSCIOUSNESS consisted of became sort of a larger-than-life issue – and as a result it took on both official and unofficial definitions as all larger-than-life issues do. In the official sense, it was generally defined via five ways:

"Awareness, especially of something within oneself; also, the state or fact of being conscious of an external object, state, or fact;

"The state of being characterized by sensation, emotion, volition, and thought-mind;

"The totality of conscious states of an individual;

"The normal state of conscious life;

"The upper level of mental life as contrasted with unconscious processes."

The definition of "the normal state of conscious life" can right away be seen as problematical. But it must be remembered that efforts to establish what the normal (and hence the abnormal) consisted of was a very big mainstream sociology-psychology project during the late nineteenth century and the first six decades of the twentieth century.

"The normal state of conscious life" definition devalued one of the earliest definitions of consciousness, i.e., "the state or fact of being mentally conscious or aware of ANYTHING."

As it then transpired, the introduction of this particular definition divided studies of consciousness into two categories –

(1) normal consciousness, and (2) abnormal consciousness –
and the constricting and deplorable effects of this division have
not yet faded away altogether.

Indeed, many individuals today agonize whether what they
do become aware of reflects normal or abnormal consciousness.
And if anything could introduce black holes regarding what
consciousness can DO, this was it.

13

Meanwhile during the twentieth century, unofficial
definitions of normal consciousness were on-going outside of
limited official dictionary definitions.

As a brief summary found in ENCYCLOPEDIA OF ESOTERIC
MAN by Benjamin Walker (1977): Consciousness is the
subjective factor that characterizes awareness, and commonly
designates the normal waking consciousness. It is a
psychological and physiological concept, as distinguished from
mind, which is largely a philosophical one.

It is the intra-psychic condition experienced by the ego or
personality during all of its self-aware activities.

Through, or because of, these activities, the ego exercises
multiple categories of consciousness:

1) perception, the apprehension of things, through the
   sense organs;
2) cognition, the understanding of what is presented to the
   senses;
3) memory, the recall and recognition of past experiences;
4) thinking, the process of reasoning, sifting, analyzing and
   making judgments;
5) feeling, or experiencing emotion and empathic states;
   and
6) willing or activity.

As illuminating as the combined six-point definition might
seem, many important thinkers considered that this portrayal of
normal waking consciousness not only defeated but also
prevented any real acquisition of knowledge about
consciousness per se.

For example, prior to World War 1, the famous German philosopher, Friedrich Nietzsche (1844-1900), deplored this line-up as an absurd over-valuation of waking consciousness – and went on to state that "the waking and rationalizing consciousness is a danger, and whoever has lived among conscious Europeans knows in fact that it is an illness."

Before his death in 1900, Nietzsche also predicted that the forthcoming twentieth century would be the bloodiest and most war-torn in human history – and which, as historians now recognize, is how it turned out to be, although no one paid any attention to Nietzsche's intuitive insight and foresight.

As another example, the modern mystic and occultist, Georgei I. Gurdjieff (1877?-1949), indicated that waking consciousness is limited consciousness. It is only a mechanical reflex, an automatic activity carried on by the neuronal, ganglionic, or cerebral systems, and almost exclusively a matter of the brain and sense organs. As such, it is properly the sphere of the neuro-physiologist and behaviorist. It has no primacy over the rest of the mind, except that it is best fitted for dealing with the practical needs of everyday life.

And, indeed, if we study what various people DO with or within their waking consciousness, there are numerous depressing occasions to wonder if waking consciousness is all there is to consciousness, or to human life itself.

Chapter Four

THE QUESTION OF THE TOTALITY OF CONSCIOUSNESS STATES OF THE INDIVIDUAL

14

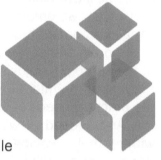

AS HAS been discussed, one of principle definitions for consciousness is given as the totality of the conscious states of the individual – but with the stipulation that "conscious states" refers exclusively to consciousness while awake.

There is no problem with the fact that the individual has conscious states. But there are difficulties with respect to what their totality consists of.

The first aspect of these difficulties is that the totality beyond the waking state remains largely rejected and/or completely unknown.

The second aspect involves certain discrepancies between the definitions of CONSCIOUS and CONSCIOUSNESS that are usually not pointed up all that clearly.

The two terms are used as synonyms. But CONSCIOUS is closely connected to whatever one becomes conscious OF during the waking state.

Although CONSCIOUSNESS can be used in the contexts of the waking state, it is more precisely understood as referring to the collective of consciousness states per se, whether or not one is conscious of them in the waking state.

15

For example, everyone experiences dreams in the sleep state. The sleep state, of course, is NOT the waking state, and so here is a state of non-awake consciousness activity that is not dependent on the criteria used to determine CONSCIOUS OF during the waking state.

The dream state clearly illustrates that individuals do possess states of consciousness in addition to what is experienced in the waking state. But, for emphasis, this is the same as saying that consciousness states exist which the individual is not conscious of during the waking state.

In fact, there are quite a number of consciousness states that carry on their activities independently of the waking state. Several of these have achieved official recognition, but many others of them have not.

Those that have are generally grouped together under the heading of the subconscious, meaning "under" or "beneath" being awake-conscious of them.

By now, there is a rather long list of subconscious activities that have achieved official or semi-official recognition. These generally include pre-conscious systems and processes that deal with and format various kinds of information BEFORE it enters the waking conscious level, with the waking conscious level usually being completely non-conscious of such goings-on.

It is now generally understood that if such pre-conscious processes did not exist, then the state of waking conscious OF would not be able to function much beyond the stimulus-response level – if that.

This is much to say, for example, that the waking conscious level would neither be able to rationalize nor deal within deductive contexts – these factors being two of the most significant hallmarks of our species.

Now, systems within an organism that process information really ought to be thought of as having some kind of consciousness. Indeed, as a suffix, NESS refers to "having the quality of."

The term CONSCIOUSNESS, then, can be thought of as referring to anything and everything that exhibits the quality of being conscious of in some form or other.

The existence of subconscious, pre-conscious information systems is now taken for granted, but their importance is certainly underrated, at least in general terms.

For those taking an interest in finding out about them, it will eventually dawn that they are larger and more extensive than whatever goes on in waking conscious OF.

Indeed, against the panorama of this larger-ness, waking conscious OF is thus only a transient wave in an infinite ocean of consciousness potentials.

Beyond what has been discussed so far are states of consciousness that have not yet achieved very much official recognition, if any.

These can generally be grouped together under the term XENOPHRENIA, taken from two Greek terms meaning "strange mind."

Chapter Five

STRANGE MIND – ITS DEEP-IN AND FAR-OUT DIMENSIONS

16

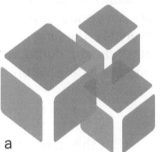

THIS AUTHOR has not been able to track down when the term XENOPHRENIA was introduced, but there is an entry for it in Benjamin Walker's ENCYCLOPEDIA OF ESOTERIC MAN published in 1977 – and which is a fascinating read overall, if only for the reason that it discusses the esoteric (hidden, concealed) meanings of various sexual organs and activities.

The word XENOPHRENIA never caught on, but it was meant as "a comprehensive term that might be applied to all those states in which the normal workaday consciousness is temporarily displaced or set in abeyance, and a different kind of awareness consciousness supervenes."

In strange mind experiencing, it seems that the fluctuating boundaries between waking conscious-of and not-conscious-of are breached, and material from the latter filters into the former.

One becomes more or less oblivious of one's surroundings. Brain memory becomes blurred or obliterated, and the systems of the individual open up to other perspectives.

Some of these perspectives are familiar, such as intuition, precognition, telepathic union, types of clairvoyance, extraordinary deduction, sudden problem solving, amplification of physical senses (especially of hearing and the tactile senses), and of awareness, etc.

Strange mind includes both the substrata and the outer

reaches of consciousness, and the individual becomes sensitive to "deep in" and "far out" dimensions.

One possible reason as to why xenophrenia never caught on is that there was a great reluctance, certainly in conventional modern scientific and psychological contexts, to admit that the mind had actual and legitimate strange mind components that could "go" both deep in and far out.

Another possible reason is that xenophrenia was overtaken and overwhelmed by the concept of ALTERED STATES – which became enormously popular.

Although no good definition for that concept yet exists, it is generally assumed that an altered state completely knocks out or suspends everyday waking consciousness, especially everyday thinking and reasoning. A good example of this is daydreaming during which one tends to lose perceptual contact with the local environment.

17

But this is not necessarily the case with respect to strange mind events and experiencing.

For example, good water dowsers hardly ever go into a complete altered state, but merely add to their everyday state a sensitivity to water underground. After all, if their everyday thinking and reasoning were suspended, they might not see the cliff ahead, or the snake, or the big tree they might collide with.

Admittedly, there are numerous strange mind experiences that do suspend everyday awake awareness, but there are numerous ones that do not. Many individuals are sensitive to electrical and magnetic activity and to subtle martial arts phenomena, to say nothing of being sensitive to sexual vibes.

Such sensitivities do not suspend everyday awake thinking or reasoning but are simply incorporated into them. Some even report having visions without missing a step in their everyday awake thinking and reasoning.

It is thus that the boundaries between mind and strange mind at least wobble a lot, and sometimes touch and integrate with each other. This is clearly the case with respect to intuition.

There are many complexities within strange-mind events. But certainly, one of the LESS complex is the sensing that one is

MORE than one has learned to think of oneself as.

The reason this is less complex is because it is undeniably the case.

Chapter Six

EXCEPTIONAL HUMAN EXPERIENCING

18

IN A CERTAIN SENSE, the twentieth century could be thought of as the century of psychology Western style, and which style was characterized by being filtered through the doctrines of philosophical materialism, a quite precise reality box, coupled with the scientific method of reductionism, another precise reality box.

HISTORICAL TIDBIT. The term PSYCHOLOGY came into existence at about 1640, and in this first incarnation it was styled as the scientific study of the soul. This new science generally retained that style until about 1842 when it was redefined as the study of the history of the mental faculties of mankind (i.e., the faculties of our species).

That incarnation did not last too long, for at about 1872, it was again redefined "as the study of the 'so-called' faculties of the mind – as contrasted to the science of physiology that studied the functions of the body."

That style endured for about four decades when psychology began to be thought of as not only the study of the mind, but of behavior. During the 1920s, it was generally restyled as the study of the mental or behavioral characteristics of an individual or group.

19

From this style arose, during the 1930s, the concept of BEHAVIORISM that was precisely defined as "A doctrine [no less] that the data of psychology consist of the observable evidence of organismic [i.e., physiological] activity to the exclusion of introspective data or reference to consciousness and mind."

If you did not quite get this, it means (1) that introspection, consciousness, and mind were dumped or discarded (much to the delight of philosophical materialists who had been working to the same end), and (2) that if a physical basis for mental activity could not be found, then such consisted of hallucinations, abnormal behavior, or a damaged brain.

This author lived through the epoch of psychological behaviorism, and witnessed its astonishing rise in cultural power during the 1950s, the widespread ruckus it inspired, and its fall during the 1960s.

It is generally thought that it went down because it failed to produce reliable mind-control techniques – as some historians insist.

But more to the point, it also failed in addressing pertinent questions about human consciousness and the value of introspection, and which failure inspired the arising of many consciousness movements we are familiar with today.

20

Meanwhile, back in the 1920s-1930s, when the mind became a central psychological issue, no one yet knew exactly what the mind was (as is still the case).

The scientific way to approach this was, as usual, to erect hypothetical theories and models for the mind, and then to selectively search for data that corresponded to and supported the theories. Many of such quickly arose.

What this meant was that scientists were researching their theories, and not the broad scale of human consciousness and experiencing, with the additional happenstance that many forgot that their favorite theories and models were just that – i.e., just hypothetical.

In any event, selectively searching for supporting data obviated any need to compile an all-inclusive, broad-scale search for data that might flesh out the actual scope of mind and consciousness to the fullest extent possible.

It is of course understandable that many theorists were reluctant to undertake anything of the kind, largely because the more of such data obtained, the more likely their theories would get squashed.

21

It thereby transpired that no lists were ever compiled of what people, at the individual level, actually do or can experience, especially in the contexts of the strange mind.

Such a list was not compiled even in parapsychology – which clearly studies only selective aspects of the strange mind, but principally only with respect to equally selective theoretical viewpoints.

Indeed, certain fundamental parapsychology documents spend some pages identifying what parapsychology does NOT study – among which (believe it or not) are the mind, perception, and consciousness, to say nothing of Eastern knowledge regarding same.

22

There things stood, even in many consciousness movements, until 1990 when a woman named Rhea A. White appeared on the scene, and on her own steam, and on her own dime, elected to begin compiling such a list.

Born in 1931, Rhea was well equipped for such a task. She was a noted parapsychologist, bibliographer, and compiler of sources of information regarding the paranormal. She has published over seventy theoretical and experimental papers, and has authored or co-authored several books.

She was a member of the American Association of University Women, and had been on the board of trustees of the Academy of Religion and Psychical Research. She founded, in 1981, the Parapsychological Sources of Information Center, and also her PSI LINE DATABASE SYSTEM - the first computerized database of parapsychological literature.

It is important to note that in parallel with her PSI interests, she evolved a deep curiosity about the creative processes. This ultimately enabled her to achieve a unique overview of the many functions of human consciousness – such processes being the chief hallmark of exceptional human consciousness at work.

At the age of twenty-six, she was on the founding council of the Parapsychological Association set up in 1957 and later served as its president during 1984. In her presidential address at the time, she made a rather eye-blinking and daring suggestion: she urged parapsychologists to halt all experimentation until they knew more about the experiences people had always been and still were reporting.

Well! As already discussed, the very idea of what PEOPLE (i.e., you, me, they, anyone, everyone) actually experience within some aspect of perceiving consciousness had long been beyond the pale of social, sociological, and scientific interest – including parapsychological interest. And, in general, this is still the case as these precious pages are being written.

However, as many have discovered, it is difficult to stand in the way of a really determined woman, because if (as first choice) they cannot get considered hearings from elsewhere, they are likely (as second choice) to go solo and undertake take the fight upon themselves.

Going solo, in 1990 she began integrating her broader overviews under the general rubric of Exceptional Human Experience (EHE). In 1994, via the Worldwide Internet, she founded the Exceptional Human Experience Network.

Thereby, for the FIRST TIME in human history, an open call went out to individuals everywhere asking them to describe and report the exceptional experiences they became conscious of beyond their everyday, normal, workaday, average, usual waking consciousness. In presenting this superlative humanizing open call to people everywhere, Rhea surely numbers among the most remarkable of women and men.

Her Network-database now includes several hundreds of such reports, and her compiled list of EHEs to date describes just over 330 broad classes of such potential experiences – the whole of which cannot be provided herein, but can be accessed via the Network's Website at:

www.ehe.org

In discussion with Rhea, she completely agreed that exceptional experiences and strange mind products are similar in origin and nature.

But she wishes to clarify (correctly so) that exceptional experiences reflect potentials for cognitive linking to capacities or aspects of one's higher consciousness potentials not previously imagined possible, and that the task is then to integrate with the expanded sense of self which often has a life-changing impact.

This is a subtle but highly significant point that is easily missed, and so it deserves a short elaboration.

Strange mind events happen all of the time, and it is because of this that psychical and parapsychological researchers during the modern period undertook to study them as odd laboratory specimens of such. This was all well and good as far as it went. But it ultimately turned out that there was a general failure to consider the events in human consciousness contexts. This failure disabled consideration not only about why and wherefrom the events occurred, but also about what happened to those who experienced them after doing so.

As Rhea describes, strange mind events are simply anomalies or oddities when they first occur. But if the experiencers integrate with any of the manifold meanings implicit in the events, this increases or expands one's sense of consciousness identity and one's sense of life within the higher human potentials the events revealed. It is this integration activity that converts strange mind events into consciousness-transforming "exceptional human experiences."

But it may as well be observed that strange mind events and EHEs are formats of consciousness – and thus her list of potential exceptional experiences acts as a beginning introduction to the fuller extent or spectrum, or innate motherboard, of human consciousness.

For the purposes of this book, it is revealing to take a look at some of the more extensive forms of consciousness that many report experiencing:

Cosmic consciousness
Gaia or Earth experience
Global consciousness
Human Species consciousness
Genetic memory
Peace beyond understanding

Immortality, experience of
Inter-species communication
Ancestor encounters
Transformational experience
Exceptional energy experience
Exceptional human performance
Human-machine interaction
Noble acts - witnessing or performing
Martial arts exceptional experience
Out-of-body experience
Peak performance
Empathy and Telepathy
Unitive experience
World-Wide Web experience
Sports exceptional experience
Electrical sensitivity
Bilocation experience
Aura sensing
Sense of presence
Charisma sensing
Guardian angel encounter
Emanations
Helper encounter
Illumination
Kundalini awakening
Transcendent emotions
"Aha" experience
Lucid dreaming
Déjà vu
Intuition
Self-realization
Clairvoyance
Life review
Precognition
Diagnosis via ESP
Empathy sensing
Microscopic vision
Inspiration
Pre-natal experience
Numinous dream

Sense of immortality
Synchronicity sensing
Invulnerability experience
Plant-human experience
ET encounter
Post-death experience
Divine encounter
Angel encounter
Sense of life continuity

Chapter Seven

THE QUESTION OF THE ACTUAL EXTENT OF CONSCIOUSNESS

23

IT IS USEFUL to review the two major definitions for the term EXTENT:

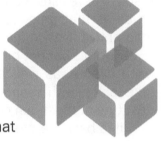

1) The range or distance over which something extends; and
2) The amount of space-time that something occupies.

Those two definitions are of course related to the term EXTEND which has several nuances: to spread or stretch; to stretch out to the fullest length; to cause to reach; to cause to be of greater area or volume; to increase the scope, meaning, or application of; and to stretch out in distance, space, or time.

24

If one takes the time, say a few years of it, to review the literature of consciousness, it can be discovered that some have experienced it as infinite, while others have experienced it at least as oceanic, especially with regard to distance, space, or time.

On the other hand, general or average experiencing of consciousness among individuals can be variable, ranging from small to big, as it were. It is this small-to-big aspect of consciousness that implies that consciousness does have extents, but also is involved with a range.

For clarity here, range is one of the pivotal words whereby the extent of anything can be discussed. One of the basic definitions of RANGE refers to "the difference between the least and greatest of an attribute or its variable of frequency distribution," and which meaning is comparable to the definition of SCOPE, i.e., "space or opportunity for unhampered motion, activity, or thought."

25

It is obvious that many individuals do not experience consciousness as infinite or even as having a large range. As a result, there are commonplace, prosaic, and slightly elitist attitudes that propose to explain that such individuals do not inherently have too much consciousness to begin with.

But this cannot be the case at all – simply because strange mind events, as well as exceptional human experiencing can take place with respect to anyone, including those allegedly destitute of too much consciousness.

It is because of such widespread experiencing, through the centuries and in all walks of life, that a full spectrum of consciousness is innate in our species, and hence innate in all individuals born of it – although large parts along the innate range of consciousness can remain inactive and latent because of circumstances subsequent to birth.

26

If one wishes to consider the extent of consciousness per se, it seems that it can tentatively be broken apart (for the purposes of this book at least), into at least three major aspects.

First, there is the matter of so-called "average" or "usual" consciousness at the human individual level. With respect to this aspect, it can be seen, based on very strong evidence, that consciousness of individuals is composed of at least three categories – waking consciousness, subconscious consciousness, and strange-mind consciousness.

Second, there is the matter of consciousness potentials of the human species entire, and for which hardly any organized research has ever been initiated.

Third, and in the very larger picture of all things, there is the matter of experiencing various formats of universal or cosmic consciousness for which there is compelling evidence regardless of what various societal enclaves think of it.

27

Certain events or happenings within strange-mind contexts can sometimes allow individual consciousness to somehow interface with the second and third major aspects of consciousness per se.

An example of the third aspect, individuals sometimes gaze at the stars glittering in the enormous panorama of the night sky – and suddenly experience the feeling of being a part of or actually belonging to the Out There.

Indeed, during the last thirty years, this author has had the opportunity of giving many lectures, and he sometimes asked how many among the audience "feel they belong out there." Many hands were raised, indeed many more than might be expected.

In the past, this kind of thing was sometimes referred to as mystical, i.e., as "having a spiritual meaning or reality that is neither apparent to the senses nor obvious to the intelligence."

There is a two-fold problem with this definition of MYSTICAL, in that it was apparently written by someone who had not had the experience – i.e., that the feeling of belonging to the "out there" IS apparent to the senses, or it would not be sensed; and, that it is also obvious to the intelligence because it takes some modicum of intelligence to recognize the difference between the here and the out there.

Of course, what kinds of senses and intelligence are involved in this are not exactly understood, but the experiencing IS understood by those who do experience it.

28

To be fair regarding the definitions of MYSTICAL, there is another one that reads: "based upon intuition, insight, or similar subjective experience."

It can be seen that intuition, insight, or similar subjective experiencing do NOT fall within the scope of everyday waking consciousness but seem more to belong to strange-mind activities that occasionally fluctuate in and out of the waking state, the sleep-dream state, and various types of meditative states.

In any event, the two definitions of MYSTICAL belong to a time when strange-mind experiencing as a whole was thought not to be really real or to have any real importance.

Yet, if one studies the history of human inventiveness, it is clear that a large part of what has come into undeniable reality has descended out of intuition, insight, or similar subjective experiencing, including sleep-dream states – i.e., out of strange mind experiencing.

29

With respect to the second major aspect of consciousness within which individuals sometimes experience the consciousness of the human species entire, that aspect also sometimes allows or permits some kind of experiencing of the consciousness of other species as well.

This particular aspect of the extent of consciousness will perhaps be best understood by various kinds of animal lovers and individuals having the remarkable green-thumb, and even by environmentalists.

To such individuals, this kind of consciousness interfacing is wondrous and is generally thought of not only as exceptional but NECESSARY for any number of increasingly important reasons.

30

The extents and facets of consciousness discussed so far are broadly experienced, and have been for quite a long time.

So, it cannot overall be said that knowledge vacuums in human consciousness exactly exist regarding them. However, it can be said that such experiencing generally remains unofficial in the face of knowledge that is accepted as official within the accepted realities of conventional contexts.

It is easy enough to discover that conventional contexts, especially modern philosophic and scientific ones, have rejected interest in what might comprise research into the extent of consciousness.

This rejection is not only implicit but has been made obvious and conclusive via many documents and statements emanating from the collective thinking of important philosophic and scientific sources.

With respect to this, it must be established that thinking, per se, is some kind of a format of consciousness – and collective thinking is, shall we say, a larger format of it incorporating the thinking of all who join into and with it.

Indeed, the more who join into it, the more collective, conventional, official, and apparently real it becomes – to those incorporated at least.

Further, conventional knowledge conglomerates, even though they come and go through time and history, have the place they do within the more fuller scope of human consciousness overall.

If there are any vacuums of knowledge within human consciousness overall, well then, such IS the case, if contrasted to the fuller and quite probably extensive panorama of consciousness itself.

Individuals might anyhow experience aspects of the larger extent of consciousness. But human consciousness overall is clearly a collective consciousness of the species entire.

Chapter Eight

THREE ALLEDGED MAJOR PARTS OF EVERYONE

31

ALTHOUGH future inquiry might add to them, it has been generally agreed for some time that all people have three major parts. These are described as the body, the emotions, and the mind, each of which has many subsidiary parts too numerous to discuss here.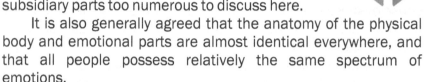

It is also generally agreed that the anatomy of the physical body and emotional parts are almost identical everywhere, and that all people possess relatively the same spectrum of emotions.

When it comes to the mind part, however, there is very little general agreement about it. To be sure, it is widely understood that everyone has the mind part, but after that it can become difficult to see that it is relatively the same in everyone.

One of the problems involved with this is that there is great deal of historical evidence showing that the mind parts of some do not want the mind parts of others to be the same as their own.

As but one rather gross example, history does show that the overlords of slaves, laborers, and the working classes do not want the mind parts of those creatures to be the same. Furthermore, even if those creatures do have the mind parts, they are not supposed to use them in ways that might challenge the mind parts of the overlords.

32

One good way to help establish and ensure this distinction was discovered way back at Day One. The mind parts of the working creatures must be kept as dumbed-down, as ignorant, and as illiterate as possible, this strategy being the fundamental basis for control of the mind parts.

Another way was to forbid too much uncovering of knowledge as to what the mind parts actually consisted of and how they work. This particular activity has been so popular throughout the successive centuries that even the overlords ended up in the dark with respect to what their own mind parts consisted of and how they work.

Viewed from the perspective of the overlords, it was a small price to pay if it helped maintain the principal distinction discussed above.

33

At about 1750, with the advent of the Industrial Revolution, it was realized that workers needed to become literate enough to read instructions about how to operate machines that held great promise for capitalistic entrepreneurs and overlords. Thus, reading and writing literacy had to be extended to male workers, although such was in general withheld from females for about another hundred years or so.

As the freedom to read and write became more and more widespread, the distinction between overlords and workers still needed, somehow, to be maintained. The way to maintain this was to prevent, or at least confuse, knowledge about what the mind parts consisted of and how they worked.

Indeed, if the literate could discover knowledge about their mind parts, then they might elect to develop them, and thus not only rise above their station in life, but, of all dreaded things, become mind-power equals to the overlord classes.

34

Thus arose the pertinent question not only of what the mind parts consisted of, but also the question of the possible, even probable, powers of those parts. One can see the difficulties here, and it is these difficulties that came to characterize mind-research as it was conceptualized and styled during the nineteenth and twentieth centuries.

In the contexts of THAT research, but for reasons that are nowhere clearly documented, it was decided that the brain was the seat of the mind.

Although many disagreed with this from the start, it became a reality-box convention to think that the mind was IN the brain, and the idea persisted even after the leading brain researcher of the twentieth century, Wilder Penfield (1891-1976), scandalized his scientific peers by concluding that the mind was not in the brain.

35

Now, the brain (and its anatomy) belongs to the physical part of the individual. Like the other physical organs (heart, liver, intestines, glands, etc.) everyone has one, and in this sense, it would seem that the brain (and hence the mind) would operate with a regularity more or less like the other physical organs do.

The fact is that the brain, unless it is damaged, DOES operate with regularity some or even most of the time. And so, during the early twentieth century it transpired that conventional brain-mind research accepted those aspects of mind that apparently conformed to the regularity of the brain.

The basic reason for this was that those aspects that did conform to the regularity of the brain had a PHYSICAL explanation. This justified the preconception that aspects of mind for which there could be found no physical basis were mere hallucinations or worse.

36

There is little doubt that evolving brain research altogether has been wonderful, and has yielded extremely important knowledge packages.

But there are two slight facts about the mind part(s) of everyone. First, the MIND part, as contrasted to the physical workings of the brain, seldom operates with any regularity even some, much less most of the time, and that everyone experiences mind-things that cannot anywhere be fitted into the regularity of the physical brain.

Take telepathy as but one of many examples. The real

existence of telepathy is quite widely experienced and very well documented, and any average Joe or Jane at least tacitly acknowledges its existence.

But there are some interesting facets of telepathy that usually escape notice.

For one thing, it is almost always referred to as mind-to-mind, not as brain-to-brain. For another thing, telepathy can occur when the brain is in low activity, and when the neo-cortex is attenuated and asleep. As is so far known, the cortex is most certainly the seat of perceptual activity, but only when the individual is awake, and the cortex is working with its perceptual regularity.

The existence of telepathy indicates that there is an edge, as it were, of the mind part that doesn't exactly correspond to the physical part.

In fact, there are likewise very many mind aspects that exist, which individuals actually experience even if only occasionally, but which cannot be fitted into any physical frame of reference so far known.

Chapter Nine

THE AVOIDANCE OF WHAT PEOPLE ACTUALLY EXPERIENCE

37

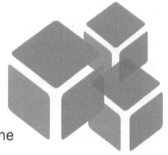

IT WOULD SEEM that human knowledge could largely be based on what people actually experience, especially via their mind parts, which are generally admitted as constituting the seat of human experiencing.

However, if one examines various cultures, it is possible to discover that each of them have and depend upon their traditions, which is more precisely to say, their DIFFERENT tradition, and most of which have treated mental phenomena in various, and often contrasting, ways.

Included in such traditions are two principal factors which are: (1) particular ways of thinking and doing things that are deemed acceptable; and (2) particular ways of thinking and doing that are, well, taboo, and are thus beyond the pale of acceptable experiencing.

There is also a third factor. This involves the two-fold idea that some are permitted to experience more than others, while the others should experience only what is allotted to their class or station in life, with the proviso that the allotment is to be very small and narrow, or at least very superficial.

Although entire cultures and societal orders can be built upon these three factors, these factors make it quite difficult to discover what humans do, might, can, or could experience.

In varying degrees, these three factors can be seen as present throughout recorded history, and most clearly so during the early twentieth century, which was early heralded as the dawning of the Age of Progress, especially that of scientific progress, which would, by the end of the century, have established something quite near a utopian world.

It was thus that almost everything came under some kind of scientific scrutiny and study, with one exception. This exception had to do with what the human species is capable of experiencing as a whole, and thus what all individuals, as members of the species, might experience within, well, the totality of their experiencing potentials.

38

During the early years of the Age of Progress, it was established that individuals could experience a wide spectrum of awareness. But the scientific research interest focused on what constituted "normal" and "abnormal" experiencing – with the latter experiencing once more being beyond the pale of proper and acceptable.

Of course, it would take a rather large project to discover what billions of individuals do experience, and so it was easier to take much smaller "samples" of experiencing, and then to see if the results fitted into the predetermined normal-abnormal categories.

39

The establishment of the normal-abnormal categories can be thought of as rather theoretical in nature, and so what was actually being "scientifically" researched was which of the small samples fitted best with the normal-abnormal theory.

Today, it is of course understood that the normal-abnormal theory was somewhat of a silly one. But it does need to be remembered that it had tremendous scientific and intellectual clout during the early and middle decades of the twentieth century, and echos of that clout have yet not entirely faded away.

However, there were two notable results of the normal-abnormal theory.

The first was that it established modern scientific contexts for the ages-old traditional ones that demarcated between acceptable and taboo experiencing.

The second result was a sort of black hole in modernist versions of human experiencing, in that science proper ended up knowing hardly anything about the totality of human experiencing, and even knowing less about it than was known before the scientific age of progress began.

40

Indeed, there are remnants of some pre-modern, pre-scientific cultures (Australian aborigines, American Indian, Eskimo, Hawaiian kahunas, and Siberian, Chinese, and African shamans, etc.) that know a great deal about what humans can experience.

There are some language problems, however, plus a great vacuum of cognitive realizing on the parts of the moderns, scientific or otherwise.

PART TWO

BLACK HOLES AND KNOWLEDGE VACUUMS

Chapter Ten

DISTINCTIONS BETWEEN BLACK HOLES AND KNOWLEDGE VACUUMS IN HUMAN CONSCIOUSNESS

41

THE ISSUES surrounding knowledge vacuums in consciousness are far easier to discuss than those pertinent to black holes, so the former will be considered first. Ultimately, however, it will be seen that knowledge vacuums and black holes can segue into and out of each other, and so some basic distinctions between the two need to be clarified.

It seems that the existence of knowledge vacuums in consciousness is easier to grasp because of a familiar and even notorious reason. Although individuals, or groups of them, might feel they don't exactly have knowledge vacuums, OTHERS can observe that they do, and such others often take delight in pointing them out.

Of course, everyone has to operate and function within the contexts of the knowledge packages they have possession of. But even so, it can be thought, in the bigger picture of all things, that everyone has some kind of knowledge vacuums – even including intellectuals of high visibility who portray themselves as fully or abundantly replete with up-to-date knowledge packages.

42

One of the problems is that knowledge is always a cumulative thing, and hence new knowledge packages can be discovered all of the time – except in the cases of various social or societal structures that do not want new knowledge to be discovered.

Once again, history records many examples of not only the discovery of new knowledge packages, but various kinds of social resistance against them, so much so that it could be said there has been, and still is, an unidentified on-going war between old and new knowledge packages - especially if the latter suggest that a social-changing paradigm shift might get underway.

Many writers have discussed the fact that new knowledge, if significant enough, engenders paradigm battles. But the discussions tend to focus on the contexts of the new knowledge only.

So, it tends to escape notice that the battles are not exclusively about the new knowledge, but also about, and perhaps principally about, collisions of reality boxes. As will be discussed ahead, these are, of course, self-limiting reality manifestations formatted within human consciousness per se. But this is the same as saying that knowledge, whether new or old, is not the principal factor involved.

The general idea about knowledge is that it somehow has to be intellectually aligned in ways that are understandable to whomever is undertaking such an acquisition.

There is always a great deal of knowledge available, but segments of which are not acquired largely because they cannot be fitted into this or that pre-existing reality box.

This is the same as saying that knowledge itself is not the central problem with regard to accessing it.

Everyone develops some kind of basic reality box, usually early in life. Henceforth, knowledge that fits into the reality box can become more easily understandable, while knowledge, or even mere information, which cannot easily be fitted in will be dealt with differently.

The acquisition or rejection of knowledge is therefore a reality-box issue, and not simply one of knowledge itself. It can therefore be said that knowledge vacuums belong to consciousness that is being filtered through reality boxes.

In any event, it can be pointed up that perhaps everyone is in possession of knowledge vacuums about the fuller nature of consciousness, simply because not too much is known about it, whether for ugly, naive, or innocent reasons.

43

Something of the same can be said about black holes in consciousness, and which, too, are reality-box problems.

A basic distinction between knowledge vacuums and black holes in consciousness may only be one of magnitude with respect to how each impacts on others.

On average, those with knowledge vacuums can get along in their lives one way or another, and most impacts, if they occur, usually reflect on self.

However, as they are envisioned in this book, black holes in consciousness can have impacts on others, and this is entirely a different matter.

44

"Black hole" is an astronomical description for a celestial object tentatively thought to be a burned-out star that has collapsed to become so dense that it would trap anything that comes near it, including light.

If a black hole exists and traps light, then there is no way to see it, because sighting anything, even via telescopes, is due to light emanating of reflecting from it.

As early as 1967, it was suggested that a black hole might be detectable if it was drawing matter from a nearby normal star. It further had been suggested that where a gas was being drawn from a star, the gas might be sufficiently hot to emit x-rays.

In 1972, it was discovered that unusual objects orbiting other stars were emitting x-rays, and the existence of black holes was considered as confirmed.

It is theorized that the material being drawing in from a close companion most likely would form a disk that rotates about the black hole. The disk would not be steady or pulsed but would have rapid uneven fluctuations as it was being drawn in and consumed.

Astronomical black holes have been given a fair amount of science fiction treatment, and fictional star pilots always need to be alert in order to avoid getting sucked into them. For whatever gets sucked into a black hole ends up never being seen again.

45

Seizing upon the astronomical term for use in this book turns it into a metaphor, because there would at least be a poetic similarity between celestial black holes and black holes in consciousness.

In any event, when discussing black holes in consciousness with others, everyone nodded and chuckled, and without further ado understood what was meant at least in general.

This widespread response became interesting in itself, for it implied the existence of some kind of awareness that various human formats of consciousness do have black holes in them.

46

Speaking in the ideal, it can be theorized that pure, unadulterated, and complete human consciousness would not have black holes in it.

But if such consciousness could exist, then it would at least have to incorporate the three realms of consciousness outlined in the preceding section – and probably more.

Generally speaking, in metaphoric terms, a black hole in human consciousness could not directly be recognized as one, but otherwise could be recognized by virtue of what is being sucked into it.

47

If the idea that knowledge equals light is combined into the black hole metaphor, then the black hole sucks in the light or illumination of knowledge, and such is thereafter never seen again unless it somehow emerges once more in the future. There are many historical examples of this.

For instance, it was known in ancient times that the Earth

was round and orbited the sun. But during the so-called "dark age" of human knowledge, it was held that the Earth was flat and that the sun somehow made its circle over and beneath it. Many seeking to reaffirm the ancient knowledge were burnt at the stake if they did not recant.

For that matter, as late as modern progressive times, many of those experiencing what was deemed "abnormal" were treated rather harshly, and sometimes were submitted to extreme electroshock "therapy" in order to bring them back to their "normal" senses.

Even as this book is being written, there exist certain large and small sociological groupings that seek mental and physical termination of whatever or whomever does not fit into their preconceived "norms" – or, as it now can be said, into their reality boxes.

48

But more bluntly speaking, black holes in human consciousness can best be recognized by virtue of their high body counts and associated collateral damage, both of which can be quite extensive, and all of which is sucked into such holes, never to be seen again.

History is rather rich with centuries of this kind of thing, and it is worthwhile to example one such early instance of it, although doing so might make one's head to ache a little.

The ancient Assyrian king, Ashumasirpal II (883-859 B.C.), is remembered by historians as one of the conceptual founders of the centralized state, and who conquered other peoples who were incorporated into his.

Sounds familiar, doesn't it?

When in the 1840s at the ancient site of Numrud the ruins of his extensive palaces and temples began to be excavated by early modern archaeologists, very numerous artefacts, tablets, and monumental sculptures of colossal, winged bulls and mammoth bearded torsos were unearthed.

These undeniably impressive sculptures were ultimately dragged to various European and British museums where they have been widely admired ever since as eloquent and poetic examples of the king's greatness.

The unearthed tablets, however, could not at first be deciphered, but when it became possible to do so, many of them were found to contain information of the king's activities caused by him to be recorded, presumably for posterity.

On one such tablet, the king's own words with respect to some other king he conquered were recorded as follows:

"I built a pillar over against his city gate and I flayed all of the chiefs who had revolted, and I covered the pillar with their skin.

Some I walled up within the pillar, some I impaled upon the pillar on stakes, and others I bound to the stakes about the pillar . . . And I cut the limbs off the officers, of the royal officers who had rebelled.

Many captives from among them I burned with fire, and I took many as living captives. From some I cut off their noses, their ears, and their fingers, of many I put out their eyes. I made one pillar of the living and another of their heads, and I bound their heads to tree trunks around the city. Their young men and maidens I burned in the fire. Twenty men I captured alive, and I immured them in the wall of his palace . . . The rest of their warriors I consumed with thirst in the desert of the Euphrates."

Well, now! Although some writers opine that Ashumasirpal's statement merely reveals his "sadistic streak," it can be wondered, in the contexts of this book at least, what he and his participating minions were using for a reality box.

It might also be wondered if the body counts of this gross and bitterly cruel ravage were actually necessary.

In any event, history records that before and after him such activities have more than occasionally been standard operating procedure – and, as submitted herein, are representative of black holes in human consciousness, justified under the guise of somehow being politically expedient.

Indeed, we can move ahead from Ashumasirpal's time to the decades of the twice great Mongolian conqueror Jenghiz (or Genghis) Khan (1167?-1227), who amassed and ruled one of the largest land empires ever known.

It ultimately extended westward across China and ultimately bumped up against East European nations. For this achievement, Jenghiz is not only remembered as the Great Khan, but, somewhat confusingly, as the Greatest Scourge of all time since he indeed effected genocidal body-counts of monumental proportions.

We can also move ahead to the time of Hernán Cortés (1485-1574), the Spanish conquistador who, on behalf of the king of Spain, invaded Aztec Mexico with the sole intent of seizing the vast amounts of gold alleged to be therein.

However, once into Aztec territory, Cortés and his men encountered (to say nothing of victims of internecine Aztec wars) hundreds of temples in whose precincts hundreds of human victims had their hearts pulled out almost on a daily basis for no other reason than to placate the numerous Aztec deities or, of all things, to ascertain omens about the future. The Cortés gold searching expedition took great exception to this activity, and Cortés ultimately utilized it as justification for colonizing Mexico on behalf of Spain.

Meanwhile, back at Cortés's native ranch of Spain, the Spanish and other medieval European Inquisitions, begun in 1233, were still ongoing, not to be abolished until 1834. Of these Inquisitions, the Spanish one was the most cruel and infamous with respect to its body-counts.

But even so, the combined Inquisitional body-count over time achieved upwards of thousands upon thousands of victims – all merely on behalf, it needs to be mentioned, of little more than ideological difficulties.

49

Now, one might think that this kind of thing belongs in the past, but if we come forward into the twentieth century, we find that it was not at all over with.

Aside from the extensive body counts, and additional collateral damages, of the First and Second World Wars in Europe, and of the Korean, Vietnam, and other lesser wars, it is also recorded that exterminations otherwise took place not only in Germany, but also in the Soviet Union, in China, and in South-East Asia, and even in various parts of South America, the combined rough total body count of which is at least in the upper hundreds of millions if not touching a billion.

As some daring historians now observe, the twentieth century (AKA the Age of Scientific Progress) is a stunning example of such black holes that altogether sucked in something like a billion plus human lives, etc., all never to be seen again, or even remembered all that much.

Chapter Eleven

THE CONVENTIONAL DISPOSAL OF CONSCIOUSNESS AND ANY BLACK HOLES AND KNOWLEDGE VACUUMS IN IT

50

THE QUESTION of black holes in human consciousness not only refers to decidedly ugly issues but is also a rather ticklish and sometimes volcanic project. However, if the full extent of human consciousness is to be opened up and studied as a project, then it is of little use to avoid such issues.

One possible reason for the ticklish nature of this project is that while some are quick to point up black holes in the consciousness of others, they, themselves, feel they do not have anything of the kind.

Another possible reason has to do with the widespread assumption that some have more consciousness than others – which might be amended more specifically to say that some higher few have more of it than the collective mass of the lower orders comprised of all others.

The extent of this assumption often includes two companion ideas: that one cannot expect to find too much consciousness, if any, in the lower orders; and, if increases in consciousness somehow emerge in THOSE orders, then this is something to worry about.

51

Still another possible reason has several facets. Many are not exactly sure about what consciousness is, and so they look to others to find out more about it.

As might be expected, this gives the others the opportunity to determine what consciousness should and should not consist of – and also who should or should not have more or less of it.

If, as many hope, MORE consciousness somehow equates to MORE awareness and perception, then (and as might be guessed) access to more extensive consciousness by just anyone, or everyone, becomes a problem within social contexts that depend upon an unequal distribution of access to it.

It thus becomes important within such social contexts to limit dependable information about the real extent of human consciousness.

52

There are many ways to establish limits. But one rather traditional way is, first, to understand that individuals will adapt to information that is held as official (conventional) within this or that societal framework.

This kind of adapting is rewarded with social approval, and it gives the adaptee a sense of belonging to the social framework.

But a second companion factor is also important. This has to do with understanding that individuals are far less likely to WANT to adapt to information about the extent of consciousness if such information is kept in some kind of unofficial state – i.e., kept in limbo or as taboo.

Adapting to unofficial information serves to place the adaptee outside of approved information contexts, and all THAT might ultimately entail.

Since it is broadly understood that most feel secure within the contexts of approved information, they will not aspire too much to adapt to unofficial information even if it is otherwise accessible.

It can thus transpire through the historical generations that although real human experiencing of more extensive elements and states of consciousness can take place, the bulk of such information can be held in general abeyance merely by stigmatizing it as unofficial.

So, on average, few will attempt to adapt to stigmatized information about consciousness potentials.

At the individual level, doing so will erode their sense of belonging to whatever social ordering they feel they belong to. And, at the collective level, such adapting will also begin to place them outside of the social support systems they can otherwise fit into.

53

Now, what has been discussed above is not really new to many, and as such is usually referred to merely as problematical within the overall accumulation of knowledge.

But it can also be observed, as some have done, that knowledge is usually accumulated to the benefit of conventional societal frameworks that sponsor the accumulation - and which frameworks are usually opposed to sponsoring any accumulation of unofficial knowledge that might end up eroding their relative legitimacy.

In various societal orders, then, knowledge is thought of as consisting only of what is approved of as knowledge. This means that knowledge rejected and disapproved of can also exist but can be placed elsewhere than within the contexts of approved knowledge.

Whether rejected knowledge equates to black holes in knowledge is open for discussion. But the overall whole of this quite large and prevailing situation is murky and sometimes demonstrates black-hole-like overtones.

54

There is also the question of whether rejected knowledge equates to black holes in human consciousness – at least within the formats of consciousness that reject it. One therefore needs to proceed slowly and not jump to easy answers – for in the end, the answers might be greater than the questions posed.

In any event, it can easily be seen that consciousness of individuals must somehow become formatted in ways that coincide with the shared conventional consciousness of the societal groupings they live and labor within.

Because of this, the question might arise as to whether the contexts of conventional consciousness of societal groupings have black holes in THEMSELVES.

55

Some twenty-five years ago, this author had the rare opportunity of a face-to-face conversation with one of the important editors of a conventional and very prestigious mainstream magazine.

He was quite fair about acknowledging the real existence of the probable extent of human consciousness perspectives.

But he quickly added: "Real power is always vested in organized conventional formats comprised of the many, and the larger the better.

"In comparison to these great world-shaping systems, the small dither about the extent of human consciousness is nothing more than a gnat on a rat's ass."

Well! How's THAT for a reality box! It is thus that consciousness can be disposed of, not only with respect to studying knowledge vacuums and black holes in it, but also with respect to its undiscovered or unrealized potentials.

56

Human history can be interpreted in numerous ways, depending on what is recorded of it. What is recorded on average tends to proclaim the greatness of certain individuals along with the events and monuments they inspired. In keeping with their destructions and atrocities, wars and other kinds of holocausts are also recorded as great victories by those who won them.

Some few heroic fatalities are also remembered, sometimes with statistical mention of the additional and nameless masses of other fatalities.

However, the statistical dead are soon forgotten in most

histories, largely because they ARE dead and have passed into historical oblivion, and so who they were is of little importance.

It is thus that human history can largely be made to reflect feel-good versions of greatness and triumph over forces and situations, but which, like the nameless dead, are forgotten or minimalized because they, too, are "dead" and have also passed into historical oblivion.

57

Another way to view history is to tabulate how much of it actually involves little else than territorial and/or ideological expansions, both of which ultimately bestow social power, and hence control of wealth and resources.

In this view of history, and as often pointed up by some historians, ideological expansionisms frequently play the largest role, essentially because such can be utilized to justify territorial and social-power grabs. Indeed, numerous historians, anthropologists, and sociological analysts have commented on this.

58

However, there are two factors that are not often commented on, the first of which is quite obvious. It is clear enough that the more successful a given ideological expansionism becomes, the more reality and relevance is attributed to it.

But, second, it is hardly ever made clear that all ideologies are, in the first place, mental in nature, and are therefore products of mind-consciousness.

The importance of this can achieve luminosity simply by wondering where ideological constructs originate or come from. It is abundantly obvious that the physical elements of the world do not tell humans what to think about them. Thus, what is to be thought about anything must everywhere, and in all times, be contributed by members of our species, whomever they turn out to be.

59

Seen in the light of the foregoing, it appears that most of human history consists of sagas of the ups and downs of ideological thinking, of their on-going conflicts, and their positive or negative results.

Most already understand this, of course. But what seems to escape too much notice is that all ideology thinking reflects only assumed versions of reality. Even this is somewhat understood today via the contexts of virtual reality, wherein realities (i.e., reality box ideas) can be put together in any way one wants.

In this sense, however, what seems completely to escape notice is that a larger, perhaps the largest, part of history is the story of the ups and downs of on-going human mind-consciousness itself, together with knowledge vacuums and often deplorable black holes within it.

60

One of the problems central to all of this is that while there has always been much ado and vigorous activity about ideological matters, it seems that no one has wondered why our species can produce so many of them, and continue to do so everywhere, and down through all subsequent generations. Indeed, there are no peoples anywhere, and in any time, which have NOT produced such.

Seen in this larger-picture perspective, there is only one possible explanation – that the human species possesses innate mind-consciousness equipment, so to speak, for building ideological frameworks.

However, what IS innate throughout our species has hardly ever been inquired into, simply because most ideological frameworks, once established as such, prove reluctant to consider such a vista larger than their own.

PART THREE

HUMAN SPECIES INNATE

Chapter Twelve

MIND AS A BLANK SLATE

61

FOR MANY CENTURIES, who knows how many, it was generally accepted that "human nature" existed. This "nature" was composed of manifold factors individuals were born with, including certain innate "ideas" (or constructs) such as mathematical ideals, moral certitude, eternal truths, and concepts (or awareness) of the Divine.

HISTORICAL TIDBIT: During the post-Renaissance decades, however, and moving toward modern times, some important philosophers began to entangle themselves regarding the extent of innate human nature - for example, Rene Descartes (1596-1650) and Nicolas Malebranche (1638-1715) in France, and Baruch Spinoza (1632-1677) in Holland.

During this period, the English empiricist and philosopher, John Locke (1632-1704) also appeared on the scene and set about knocking down the idea that the human mind possessed innate ideas. With this project, Locke seems to have set the stage for what thereafter developed into the enormous and often volcanic battle, still on-going, between nature versus nurture.

One of Locke's basic contentions was that there are no innate ideas or principles stamped upon the mind of man and brought into the world by the soul. The mind was born a "tabula rasa," and which, after birth, could be written upon via the acquisition of experience, learning, and knowledge.

The Latin term TABULA RASA translates into English as "scraped slate." In antiquity, such slates were composed of some soft, porous material, yet strong enough to be incised with writing, after which the slate could lightly be scraped clean and therefore ready to be written upon again.

Locke's original use of "scraped slate" soon proved to be inconvenient to Western philosophers, since it implied that something had previously been written upon it, but which had been scraped clean in preparation for the new birth of the mind. This was entirely redolent of certain Eastern concepts having to do not just with birth, but also with re-birth, etc., and all that such confusions might philosophically entail.

The difficulty was soon overcome, at least superficially, by simply substituting the word "blank" for the word "scraped," with the result that the "blank slate" mind could be defined as "the mind in its hypothetical primary blank or empty state before receiving outside impressions." Please note that some modern dictionaries give THIS definition to "tabula rasa," which is not correct.

In any event, Locke indicated that we, at birth, have natural faculties or capacities to think and to reason, but that this is not the same thing as having innate ideas. In a similar fashion, he argued that we have no innate moral or practical principles, for these differ everywhere and so there is no universal agreement about them.

62

The crux of Locke's ideas turns on his concept of "idea" which he defined as "Whatsoever is the object of the understanding when a man thinks; whatever is meant by phantasm, notion, species; or whatever it is which the mind can be employed about in thinking."

Therefore, any object of awareness or of consciousness must be [in the mind] an idea, and so knowledge itself, when possessed and made the object of the mind, must be an idea. In other words, one sees not real objects themselves, but only ideas of them formed in the mind.

It is thus, according to Locke, "that ideas stand between reality and the understanding." For clarity, reality exists, of which the mind makes whatever ideas it can, and from which ideas are derived whatever understanding can be derived from the ideas.

It should be clear that Locke is pointing up that understanding of reality is not directly derived from reality itself, but via ideas of it via which some kind of understanding is achieved or not.

It is therefore the resulting understanding that STANDS IN, so to speak, for reality itself.

In other words, whatever understanding results is at least three steps removed from reality itself, set out as follows:

First, reality exists, but

Second, we perceive reality not directly, but via our mind-made ideas of it, after which

Third, we understand reality again not directly, but via our understanding derived from our ideas of it, after which

Fourth, we erect versions of reality based on understanding our ideas of it.

63

If we accept that the ideas, understandings, and resulting versions of reality thenceforth act as frames of reference, then we have, as will be discussed ahead, the basic formula for reality boxes.

64

It seems that Locke was, in essence, dealing with reality boxes, but without that concept available to him.

In retrospect, this is more or less confirmed now in that Locke, from the outset of his work, was permanently persuaded that "our understanding and knowledge fall far short of all that exists." Which, of course, is still the case today – in that various reality boxes continue to fall far short of all that exists.

65

It turned out that Locke's idea that there are no innate principles or ideas stamped upon the mind – that the mind is a blank slate – became, well, enormously popular, and still is.

One possible reason for this popularity is that the blank slate theory, in essence, meant that there were no innate species factors involved with the blank slate mind.

Since the innate mind was empty, but apparently amenable to having ideas inserted, it could be selectively nurtured or programmed with various information packages – at least some of which could serve, dare it be said, for this or that mind-control purpose.

Such had anyway been going on throughout the centuries with or without innate species factors, but Locke's version of no innate ideas quickly became doctrinaire to those many attracted to it. However, it could have been pointed up long ago that if the mind, which is innate, has no innate ideas or principles, then consciousness, which is also innate, is also empty, is also a blank slate.

66

This consideration brings up an interesting question with regard to mere survival in the physical or material sense

Why should a biological species that is innately magnificent in its smallest details issue forth with blank minds and blank consciousness which have nothing innate in them?

Chapter Thirteen

INNATE ATTRIBUTES OF THE HUMAN SPECIES ENTIRE

67

THE DEBATE BETWEEN the adherents of innate ideas and the adherents of the blank slate became better known as the NATURE versus NURTURE debate, or fracas, or Mexican standoff.

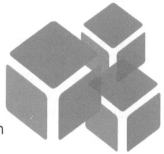

During the nineteenth and twentieth centuries the fracas became, among modernist intellectuals anyway, so extensive, intensive, complicated, convoluted, and bitter, that it can hardly be summarized in a few paragraphs. Thus, the reader might wonder why mention of the fracas was introduced into this book. Well, there are two principal reasons for doing so.

68

First, and most importantly, advocates on both sides of the debate have managed to proceed with extremely minimal, or no reference at all, to the existence of human consciousness, and which, without argument, is clearly innate in our species and in all individuals. Indeed, consciousness seems to have been considered as a kind of passive, obsequious thing having no dynamics of its own.

69

Second, two of John Locke's fundamental concepts appear

to have been entirely forgotten: (1) that mind-made ideas represent only an idea of reality, and that understanding is derived from within the contexts of the idea, but not directly from reality itself; and, (2) that our understanding, and thus our knowledge, falls far short of all that exists.

Indeed, when something new is discovered among all that exists, many previously trusted understandings quiver, explode, implode, or fall into history's dustbins.

70

There is a third reason. If one discusses the debate with numerous average or ordinary individuals, a fairly large percentage of them will ask: Why can't both exist? Why can't there be innate ideas AND a part of the mind that can be programmed via this or that socio-cultural nurturing?

These are entirely sensible questions, the portent of which is that the debate could end up in a draw, and ultimately be seen as having been ridiculous all along.

71

There is yet a fourth reason, but one that can best be grasped within the contexts of reality boxes.

While John Locke is one of the predecessors of the debate, its more clear lines seem to have been made visible by his intellectual heir, the British philosopher and economist John Stuart Mill (1806-1873).

Mill seems to have been a precocious individual and an energetic blank-slate enthusiast. So, it behooved him to opine that any idea that anything is innate in human character is one of the chief hindrances to the rational treatment of great social questions, and one of the greatest stumbling blocks to human improvement.

Mill took particular umbrage against certain intellectuals who, in his time, were advocating the idea of an "intuitional philosophy" based on the concept that the categories of reason were basically innate. Mill took great objection to this, and set about energetically attacking their theory of psychology at its root.

Mill's attacking efforts attracted squads of similar and influential enthusiasts, and from this reality-box grouping the blank-slate Theory was ultimately converted into the Blank Slate Doctrine.

The doctrine became entrenched in early modernism under the rubric of The Standard Social Science Model – better known as "social constructionism" – and which ism began to underwrite most of the great sociological experiments of the twentieth century.

Some of the experiments were merely intellectual reality-box extravaganzas, most of which ultimately flopped as times and tides came and went. But three of these, in Germany, Russia, and China, resulted in awful and morose tragedies in that they accumulated enormous body counts and equally extensive collateral damage.

72

As has already been mentioned, interest in human consciousness fell to almost nil during the epoch of the blank slate and social constructionism. After all, if the minds of individuals were merely blank slates to be written on (i.e., to be formatted by social engineering), then whether they had consciousness or not was irrelevant.

Indeed, it seems that even if individuals did have consciousness, it, too, could be written upon, because the blank slate doctrine required this concept. And so, consciousness and its potential extent remained a knowledge vacuum.

73

Now, one way to begin thinking about the probable extent of human consciousness is to examine what humans have in common outside of their cultural and societal contexts.

The principal reason for doing so is that it is now quite well understood that cultural and societal contexts work to, well, program individuals to fit into them.

Since cultural and societal contexts can differ very widely, collectives of individuals, arise each of which can seem quite different.

Most have realized this, of course, and so during, say, the last two hundred years, great interest arose, especially in anthropological and sociological studies, regarding how peoples and their social structures differed.

74

From this study, it was apparent from the outset that all cultural and societal contexts developed language usage, and so interest arose in linguistic studies as to how languages differed.

After a while, it also became apparent that although the terminology of languages did differ, most of them were similar with regard to certain systematic necessities, such as the need for nouns, verbs, adjectives, adverbs, and certain grammatical structures.

It had been understood for centuries that these necessities could be translated into their equivalents in other languages.

And so, it became possible to erect language trees and sometimes trace different languages back to their common roots.

75

It had long been thought that different languages arose BECAUSE of different environmental needs, and because of different socio-cultural traditions. Even so, John Locke was certain that men possessed a capacity for knowledge sufficient for their purposes and matters they needed to enquire into.

Since groups of people need a language in order to communicate, it was thought that languages were, at base, separately and independently built up from vocalized grunts and other monosyllable noises into some kind of vocalizing associated with meanings.

But rather recently it began to be recognized that languages more properly exist because the human species, and all individuals issuing from it, have the innate, inborn, and generic capacity for erecting language systems, and the generic capacity for adapting to any language spoken around them.

For clarity, the means that all babes born have innate language capacity, and that this capacity, in its potential, is universal throughout the species and thus transcends individuation of languages within any given separatist societal context.

76

The first recognition of this is attributed to Noam Chomsky (1928-), the American educator and linguist who taught at the Massachusetts Institute of Technology (MIT) beginning in the 1950s, and who developed a theory of generative grammar that began revolutionizing the scientific study of language.

Instead of starting with a random hodgepodge of minimal sounds, as the structural linguists had, Chomsky pointed out that all languages obey similar rules and patterns.

He ultimately demonstrated that essential grammars of individual languages are but variations on a single pattern, which he called Universal Grammar composed of verbs, objects, nouns, adjectives, etc., all of which can be assembled in different priorities, but all of which exist in even unrelated languages.

This realization began to provide clues about the innate circuitry that makes language learning possible on a universal scale throughout the species.

If the rules and patterns, i.e., basic language ideas, of language were innate, and thus embodied in innate neural circuitry, this would explain, as it was later demonstrated, why infants, practically from Day One, commence learning their local language so easily and uniformly without the benefit of later and more complex instruction.

It is now generally accepted that babes everywhere are universally born pre-wired, so to speak, for language development – for ANY language development such as Swahili, Dutch, Chinese, Finnish, Tibetan, and even English, plus many lost languages.

Thus, although languages may differ, the potential for language-making is innate and indigenous within the species entire.

Further, the potential is universal to the species and, with only small variations, is the same everywhere one goes – IF one thinks in species terms and not in terms of different societal frameworks.

77

The onset of this discovery about universal, innate language wiring soon inspired certain researchers to seek out other human activities that might be as universally wired within our species, and thus be innate within individuals, and existing before any particular societal individuating takes place.

For clarity, in the sense that it is being used in the foregoing contexts, UNIVERSAL is defined as "present or occurring everywhere," with the proviso that what is present or occurring may not be exact, but at least quite similar, with minimal local variations involving cultural style or aesthetics.

78

One of the first books to begin listing human factors that could qualify as universals appeared in 1991, via its author Donald E. Brown, under the title of HUMAN UNIVERSALS. But Brown's first list included a proviso, to wit, that it does not include "deeper universals of mental structure" that are revealed by theory and experiments.

Consciousness, undoubtedly a universal within our species entire, does NOT appear on the list, possibly because it belongs within the category of deeper, strange mind universals of mental structure yet to be addressed.

But no matter, for the list of presumed universals is very long and extremely revealing with respect to how similarly humans are innately wired everywhere, even if they do exhibit seriously different reality boxes.

79

Now, as this author was preparing to write this book, and was making an effort, in September 2002, to try to deal with the issue of human universals, fortune chanced to lend a significant hand. For on the 17th of that month, the Old Grey Lady, otherwise known as The New York Times, published, in its science section, a review of a new book, advertising it as "In Nature vs. Nurture, a Voice for Nature."

This book, by Steven Pinker, is entitled THE BLANK SLATE:

THE MODERN DENIAL OF HUMAN NATURE, and which, as the title unambiguously indicates, is a rather thundering broadside fired into the direction of the blank slate establishment.

He is Professor of Psychology at MIT, has received many awards for his teaching, and for his earlier books HOW THE MIND WORKS, and THE LANGUAGE INSTINCT.

80

This author is entirely indebted to THE BLANK SLATE, for it eased the composing of this present section. But it must be observed right away that innate consciousness is given little attention, and that term does not appear in the book's index.

Likewise, and as will be discussed later, it does seem that the human capacity to erect reality boxes is quite universal and innate, but such is also not mentioned.

But no matter again, for Pinker's book is tremendously informative, and if it is read with the lenses of reality-box construction, many of such stand forth in neon lights.

Also included as an Appendix in Pinker's book is Donald E. Brown's List of Human Universals, with updates since 1991.

The list points up some 390 innate attributes, the vast majority of which are easily recognizable in all cultural contexts throughout the human world.

The review of Pinker's book in The New York Times was exceedingly competent, and it included a short and tentative, but important, list of some basic factors now assumed to be innate in our species. By way of review in THIS book, they are:

- An intuitive engineering, used to make and understand tools.
- An intuitive physics, used to keep track of objects as they fall, bounce, or bend.
- An intuitive biology, used to understand the living world by imputing an essence to living things.
- A spatial sense and a dead reckoner tracking the body's motions.
- A number sense, based on ability to register small numbers of things exactly and to estimate larger ones.

- A sense of probability, used to estimate uncertain outcomes by tracking how common one event is in relation to another.
- An intuitive economics, used to exchange goods and calculate favors.
- An intuitive psychology, used to understand others by imputing to them a mind with beliefs and desires.
- A mental database and logic, used to represent ideas, associate one thing with another, and devise causal explanations.

This is quite a basic list with respect not only to what is universal within our species hard drives, so to speak, but also regarding what one is BORN WITH.

However, it might be noticed that each item on the list can also be associated with some form of internal intuitive consciousness, all of which are quite near the concept of strange-mind activity.

And as already mentioned, neither consciousness nor its extent has been entered into any list of what is innate to our species, although everyone has it, and without it none of the items on the list could exist.

81

This is quite a basic list with respect not only to what is universal within our species hard drives, so to speak, but also regarding what one is BORN WITH.

Chapter Fourteen

INNATE MODULES AND CIRCUITRY OF HUMAN CONSCIOUSNESS

82

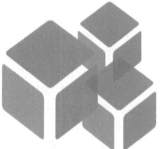

WHEN THE TERM MODULE is applied to innate human faculties and innate forms of consciousness, it becomes another useful metaphor for things that are not really understood.

MODULE is principally defined as "a packaged functional assembly of wired electronic components for use with other such assemblies."

Such assemblies automatically have to include some kind of CIRCUITRY that is defined, in its electronic sense, as "an assemblage, or hookup, of electronic elements and a complete path of an electric current usually including the source of electric energy."

Circuitry is also thought of as WIRING, defined as "a system or arrangement of wires used for electric distribution."

83

Of course, the circuitry or wiring in an assembled module has to be correctly done, and efficiently energized. If not, there will be sparks, sizzling, jolting, disruption, and possible explosions, after which the workings of the assemblage usually malfunction or grind to a halt.

Where several different kinds of modules are assembled together, so as to work in union each in its own way and functioning, it can easily be understood that malfunctioning of one module can have repercussions in all the others.

Are you getting an idea here?

84

The "born with" innate faculties referred to in the preceding chapter can easily be thought of as innate modules existing throughout our species, and which, tentatively speaking at least, can be thought of as kinds of innate consciousness potentials.

However, as previously mentioned, consciousness as an innate born-with faculty did not make it onto the list. Neither did innate faculties for memory modules that everyone does have. And so, it can be seen that a full deck of innate faculties has not yet been presented.

85

But a very important innate modular faculty DID make it onto the list, and probably for the first time ever. As described, it consists of an innate, in-born "mental database and logic, used to represent ideas, associate one thing with another and devise causal explanations."

Now, if the reader is beginning to smile (or giggle) at this in some kind of pre-knowing way, it must be remembered that the description refers to an INNATE, in-born module that can, could, perhaps, or might deal, or not deal, with various kinds of ideas, associations, and devising.

However, because this module is innate, it must, like all the other innate modules, have operating potentials that are greater than any average (so-called) use of them.

Indeed, actual human experiencing worldwide establishes that individuals, on the greater average, only deal with what they are or become conscious OF in the waking state.

But if the real existence of other states and levels of consciousness is accepted, this is almost the same as saying that even if there are black holes of consciousness relative to the waking state, such may not be equally present through and through the individual's fuller spectrum of consciousness states and potentials.

86

In any event, the author of the list of innate faculties has designated this particular in-born one as "mental."

And with this word we can now really begin smirking, largely because it has several dictionary definitions that are not entirely consistent with each other – but which can be consistent with various ideas, associations, and devising. Four of these definitions are:

1) Of or relating to mind; SPECIFICALLY relating to the total emotional and intellectual response of an individual to environment.
2) Occurring or experienced in the mind.
3) Relating to, or affected by a psychiatric disorder.
4) Relating to telepathic, mind-reading, or other occult powers.

87

Except for the fact that everyone is innately born with one, no one really knows what the mind is in any sense that is near complete.

This particular vacuum in knowledge is made further complex when it comes to the real extent of mind, especially when contrasted, as many experts have said, to the probable reality that most are using only about 10 percent or less of it, including the experts themselves.

Additionally, which of the above definitions should be applied in this or that instance depends almost entirely on which represented ideas, associations among things, and devisings are being utilized in the first place.

88

Second, the term DEVISE has two principal definitions: "to form in the mind by new combinations or applications: invent," and "to plan or plot to bring about."

DEVISE is VERY closely related to the term DEVICE, i.e., "something devised or contrived; a scheme to deceive;

something fanciful, elaborate, or intricate in design."

However, except to say that humans CAN and DO devise, invent, plot, and contrive explanations for causal relationships, one can be left wondering if such is actually an innate, in-born faculty of innate, in-born consciousness.

Well, YES, it is. For closer inspection of all that is involved with this particular consciousness module, it becomes quite apparent that innate in our species is the in-born faculty to erect reality boxes.

PART FOUR

SOME DYNAMICS OF REALITY BOXES

Chapter Fifteen

REALITY BOX

89

THIS WRITER has not been able to discover exactly when the concept of reality boxes surfaced and entered into common parlance. But one began to hear of them in the late 1960s when so many cultural conflicts came to a head, and it became apparent that not everyone shared the same ideas and perceptions of what was real.

Prior to that time, it was generally thought that people had opinions, convictions, viewpoints, and worldviews, and that these aspects could be similar, could differ, or could conflict.

It was understood that these aspects need not necessarily reflect reality – because reality (REAL reality) existed whether anyone thought so or not.

Back then, REALITY was defined as "something that is neither derivative nor dependent, but exists necessarily."

And so, one's considerations this way or that about whatever did not automatically make the considerations real either in substance or in fact.

90

During the late 1960s a sort of intellectual jump took place via which it became possible to conceptualize one's ideas as an actual modality of reality. And in that sense, it could be said that everyone had THEIR realities.

So, everyone's ideas, opinions, convictions, viewpoints, and worldviews took on vestiges of reality, even though they were totally dependent on merely thinking them so or not.

In this way, or something like it, the idea that everyone had their realities came about. This idea was one whose time had come, for it served to fill a large gap in philosophical and psychological considerations thereto.

This gap consisted of the easily ascertainable fact that although people might not have too much of a grip on what was really real or not, they tended to ACT as if they did - and it must be said that the results on others of the ACTIONS were often REAL enough.

91

However, the phrase "reality box" is yet another neat metaphor. Although the phrase is widely used today, the concept behind it is a relatively new one and there are no precise dictionary definitions for it.

Even so, it is generally understood as referring to the basic frames of reference that particular individuals automatically depend on to guide thinking processes, and out of which is constructed a mental framework of some kind that denotes "reality" for that individual.

The "box" part of the phrase is taken to mean that individuals have "realities" that are real enough to THEM, but that their considerations are limited within their "realities."

Their perception of reality is boxed in by their "realities" – which need not necessarily correspond to real realities.

Hence, individuals think and respond only in terms of their personal realities and, as a result, cannot deal with, or even sometimes perceive, realities outside of their boxes.

It is possible to be quite surprised or stunned when discovering what other peoples' realities consist of, especially if such realities are energetic and hyperactive.

Chapter Sixteen

THE COMPUTER ANALOGY

92

THE QUESTION now arises as to how it is that real reality does exist, but that individuals, and groups of them, can be in possession of personal realities that need not necessarily coincide with it.

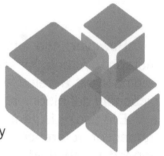

If one cogitates on this pregnant question, it might at first be concluded that personal realities are artifacts of the mind. But this is because the prevailing Image of the human is built upon only three aspects – body, mind, and, perhaps, soul – with the great working vehicle being the mind.

This Image seems serviceable enough – until definitions of body, mind, and soul are consulted.

93

HISTORICAL TIDBIT: With regard to the word MIND, the great Oxford Dictionary of the English Language indicates that it was probably taken from a Scandinavian term MYND, which meant memory.

However, the Oxford dictionary now lists just over forty definitions, and these are extended by about sixty nuances, or sub-definitions, all of which add up to a grand total of about one hundred definitions.

If, in order to become more enlightened about MIND, one undertakes to read through this grand total, one's consciousness might be overtaken by numerous confusions, resulting in boredom, torpor, or sleep.

Attributing even ten definitions to a word at least reveals imprecision. But a proliferation of definitions is also not good intellectual economy, because numerous definitions constitute a mishmash of contexts that tends to leave one unsure of what is being talked about.

In any event, the large majority of the definitions focus upon what mind IS, not upon what it DOES – and in this instance one cannot resist mentioning that it is what the mind does that is experienced at the individual level.

94

To get anywhere with the question posed at the head of this section, that question needs to be combined with the reality that individuals of our species are in possession of innate, in-born modules of faculties, the potentials of which are, say, primed for action from day one.

THIS now needs to be combined with the familiar observation that the resulting and cumulative actions differ throughout the human world, often radically so.

This could not be possible unless the innate modules primed for action could be programmed after birth with different sets of information.

95

The combining of these factors results in something quite wonderful. For it means, in theory at least, that relatively fresh human organisms could be dumped anywhere in the universe, and could format or program their innate modules with respect to information pertinent to wherever.

Human organisms that are not so fresh might not make it too well along these lines, because acquired reality-box shells and armor might be too cemented in to permit adjustments that might be advisable.

But who knows for sure, for even in Earth environments, many concretized reality boxes can groan and shift around if pressured to do so, and especially if fresh advantages are to be obtained thereby.

96

It was something of a relief when the first computers were invented in 1930, 1944, and 1946 respectively, and which were sometimes referred to as "thinking machines."

Thinking is, of course, one of the things the mind DOES, and so computers quickly became an analogy for mind, with the advantage that those crafting thinking machines at least knew precisely what was in them, and what made them tic.

At first there were only two types of computers, referred to as digital and analog.

Descriptions of the workings of the analog computer (or analog circuitry) are very interesting. But in preparation for the official description below, the term ANALOG is defined as "showing a likeness or resemblance permitting one to draw a comparison [an analogy] between them; also, inference that if two or more things agree with one another in some respects, they will probably agree in others."

As to the official definition, the Columbia Encyclopedia indicates "An analog computer is designed to process data in which the variable quantities vary continuously.

It translates the relationships between the variables of a problem into analogous relationships between electrical quantities, such as a current and voltage, and solves the original problem by solving the equivalent problem, or analog, which is set up in its electrical circuits.

Because of this feature, analog computers are especially useful in the simulation and evaluation of dynamic situations, such as the flight of a space capsule or the changing weather patterns over a certain area."

97

If the foregoing description is a bit heavy, it can be pointed up that this analog activity is also typical of inventing tools in the Stone Age; of aiming a bow and arrow and hitting the target; of executing a defensive or offensive karate chop; of succeeding with an insight, intuition, or invention; of manipulating one's way within murky power structures; and of preserving one's life in dangerous situations, etc.

One of the points of all the foregoing is that the mind is thought to act or function like an analog computer.

98

It is also understood that computers need original in-puts (of information) to be written into them, that they will thereafter function according to the analog sum of those in-puts – and only in accord with that sum.

99

Basically speaking, computers must have specific basic elements in order to function:

- A Central Processing Unit (the motherboard brain of the computer);
- Hard drives that are storage (memory) devices containing prewritten "files" of all sorts; and,
- Software programs that can be written into (i.e., installed) and be intra-processed by the hard drives and Central Processing Unit.

If the whole of all of this is in prime readiness and a "go" status, the computers will thereafter work merrily along – unless invaded by some kind of "virus" that will garble the analog circuits and their translation of relationships, and ultimately crash the system.

All of this sounds somewhat familiar, doesn't it – but not because one is up to date in the details of computerology. In any event, it is of little wonder that computers have become a somewhat apt metaphor for the human "thinking machine."

Chapter Seventeen

THE QUESTION OF THE MOTHERBOARD OF HUMAN CONSCIOUSNESS

100

THE ANALOGY of computers is frequently being utilized on the cutting edges of science, and especially in the fields of cybernetics and the design of intelligent machines.

In those fields, however, the analogy does not really refer to the mind per se. It refers to what the mind can DO and, more precisely, to how human systems sense, identify, distribute, transduce, translate, analyze, recognize, and utilize information.

As briefly discussed in the previous chapter, a computer has three basic devices that hold and process information – a central processing unit (or motherboard), hard drives, and software programs.

The motherboard is frequently referred to as the brain of the computer. Hard drives are information storage devices into which files of all kinds are already innately written, or can otherwise be written. Software consists of information packages that can be put on the hard drives.

101

Since the computer has become a popular analogy for mind, it can just as well be applied, if only hypothetically, to the total extent of human consciousness, even if that totality is largely unrecognized, or not utilized very much.

Now, human consciousness is often thought to be a somewhat random affair, especially at the individual level. At that level, the advent of consciousness in the individual is thought to arise by virtue of what the individual has experienced and thus become conscious of after birth.

In that sense, individual consciousness is seen to arise as a result of nurturing via environmental and social factors. It is very clear that such post-natal types of consciousness do exist, and on a very broad worldwide spectrum.

102

But if the advent of consciousness in individuals is linked only to post-natal contexts of nurturing via environmental and social factors, then this makes the advent and acquisition of individual consciousness an entirely random affair – and for three principal reasons.

First, there are many different socio-environmental situations that nurture exceedingly different kinds and sets of individual (and group) consciousness.

Second, the extensive plentitude of different socio-environmental situations nurture only certain kinds of consciousness, but do not nurture other kinds.

Third, all socio-environmental situations are subject to change, in that they come and go throughout time and tides of history, and so what was or was not nurtured becomes irrelevant in the end. Thus, there exists something like a permanent impermanency regarding what was or was not nurtured here and there, elsewhere, and everywhere.

103

As it turns out, however, new individuals are propagated here and there, elsewhere, and everywhere, and each of them comes in already primed with innate consciousness factors, various aspects of which can again be subjected to different socio-environmental situations.

From all of this, it can be thought that a motherboard of the permanent totality of human consciousness exists within the species entire – and that each individual has something like a "zipped file" copy of it already in place.

"Zipped file" is computerese for an information storage file that can hold VERY large amounts of tightly compressed information bits, which need to be decompressed (i.e., "opened up") in order to un-compact the bits so that they can be "read" and become actively useful again.

104

Now, there is one factor about consciousness that is quite familiar, i.e., that if various parts or categories of it don't open up then they are not experienced – so, no one is the wiser about what is in the zipped files of consciousness that could be opened up, but which could otherwise remain un-opened.

However, as discussed earlier, a wide selection of human consciousness potentials occasionally open up via altered states, the strange mind, or exceptional human experiencing, and sometimes even because of survival necessity.

And it is this that gives the vital clue that individuals possess a motherboard of total consciousness that is permanent within the species, and independent of the vagaries of socio-environmental programming and selective nurturing or non-nurturing.

105

By way of analogy, then, it could be tentatively considered that the motherboard of the totality of human consciousness exists, and that each individual has an innate zipped file copy of it.

One might then at least imagine that the zipped files have, say, something like a hundred innate ON-OFF switches or buttons each referring to circuitry of different kinds of consciousness among the whole totality of it.

It is now possible to imagine that these different kinds of consciousness need to be opened up in order to be read, or switched to the ON position, or perhaps be re-booted in order to rev up into functionality.

Well, within this imaginary context, something now depends on what has or has not become opened up or switched on.

106

In partial answer to this, it can be seen that individuals worldwide interface the best and most familiarly within the contexts of physicality.

And so it might be assumed that switches or buttons for consciousness about physical stuff are widely turned on just about everywhere throughout the total human condition, and in some kind of 10 percent way.

Next, however, might come switches and buttons having to do with opening up consciousness of intelligence, or something like it. Here, your guess is as good as anyone's, except to think that intelligence functions only to the degree it opens up within the broader spectrums and contexts of consciousness per se.

107

Next, perhaps, come the various arenas within the overall human condition, and within which individuals (and groups) do not interface too well, and which are even notoriously resistant to such interfacing.

These arenas are of course comprised of socio-environmental programming structures. These inconsistently and differently nurture or not nurture this or that, especially with respect to different reality box ideas of what human consciousness SHOULD consist of – even including its unrecognized and unknown parts.

108

It is difficult to think that such inconsistencies and differences would exist within the innate motherboard of human consciousness, largely because a significant human consciousness meltdown would have occurred not long after day one.

But it is possible that socio-environmental programming structures are somehow the equivalent of software programs that might be introduced into the innate hard drives of the motherboards of consciousness.

In any event, such socio-environmental programming

structures ARE the equivalent of reality boxes – which, at base, and in the contexts of the overall human condition, are little more than limited information management devices even at their best.

Chapter Eighteen

REALITY BOX INFORMATION FRAMEWORKS

109

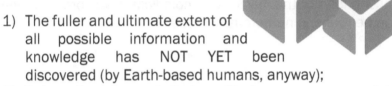

THERE ARE at least two reasons why all human reality boxes are limited:

1) The fuller and ultimate extent of all possible information and knowledge has NOT YET been discovered (by Earth-based humans, anyway);
2) It is quite apparent that reality boxes can come into existence that are based on lesser rather than greater amounts of information and knowledge.

These two factors can be mixed and recombined for a number of viewpoints. But the result of doing so is always the same.

Reality boxes are apparently made up of a smaller or larger number of information and knowledge packages that are fitted together so as to somehow form an interactive whole within whatever has been fitted together.

110

No one so far really understands why this takes place, but studies of the phenomenon link its major aspects to certain important glandular shifts that occur at given times in the progressive cadence of maturing.

It is thought that the basic processes involved commence in

infancy, during which "formative" period the child has to recognize, and somehow adapt to, at least the basics of what's what in its local socio-environmental situation.

At about the age of seven, the bio-body undergoes a series of major glandular activities that have numerous repercussions. One of these is that a sort of self-hood takes place, and the child "individuates" as a self.

Another important repercussion is that whatever the child has recognized as what's what, and imprinted upon, and so far adapted to, tends to become set and fixed.

Some scientific studies indicate that the youngster's basic character traits result, and also that these thereafter are permanent.

A full part of this "set and fixed" thing is that additional or subsequent information that fits tends to be accepted, while information that does not fit tends to be rejected. Various descriptions of this basic "psychological developmental phase" can be found in numerous sources.

111

Stepping outside of this developmental reference, all of this can be thought of as Major Event One in terms of formative reality boxes – for the youngster has now individuated as a self within local socio-environment elements and is in possession of certain set and fixed information frameworks that are pertinent to them.

These frameworks receive extensive support and reinforcement because everyone, or at least most, in such socio--environments have approximate copies of them that are mutually compatible, sharable, and interactive within the local situation. The frameworks are furthermore reinforced via devised educational processes seen as appropriate to them.

As is now generally understood, the whole of this can be examined from within many different points of view – for example, as culture making, as social conditioning, as social software programming, as the right of groups of united individuals to design and erect their own societies, and so forth.

112

Even so, within the obvious context of all of the foregoing, there are two factors or elements that seldom receive much attention.

The first of these is that when the set-and-fixing thing becomes structured into frameworks, it also has enormous relevance as to how CONSCIOUSNESS OF becomes set and fixed, and it is this that has very interesting ramifications at the individual level.

Obviously if the information frameworks of this or that local socio-environment become suitably set and fixed in their particular contexts, then elements of the totality of human consciousness that do not fit with them will at least be troublesome, if not patently unwanted or rejected.

Second, and largely via the "global village" concept, it can be seen that humans everywhere and, in all times, do erect some kind of structured information frameworks. This is usually discussed within the contexts of which framework is better, and especially who is to be empowered to be in charge of which framework, and usually at the cost of other frameworks.

113

But behind all of this is something that can be rather obvious. Information frameworks ARE established throughout our species, and it is this that implies that the capacity to do so is innate in the totality of human consciousness.

This can be put another way. Innate in our species is the capacity to erect socio-environmental software programs, even if doing so switches off, within those programs, many elements of the totality of consciousness.

Chapter Nineteen

REALITY BOX STRUCTURING OR FORMATTING

114

THE FIRST basic definition of BOX is given as "a rigid typically rectangular receptacle often with a cover."

It is usually thought that a box is something to put things into. But a box is also something to keep things outside of it. In both cases, how rigid or impermeable the box is has something to do with its ultimate efficiency – depending, of course, on what is to be protected inside from whatever is on the outside.

A human reality box is of little efficiency if what is inside it cannot be protected from leakage or adulteration by whatever is outside of it.

And so human reality boxes, in their ideal state, need to be as rigid and impermeable as possible lest their interiorized realities begin to wobble and decline in their efficiency.

115

As might be expected, and since humans erect many different kinds of reality boxes, conflicts between them can be expected to arise.

But this suggests that the resulting conflicts are really NOT conducted by human beings per se, nor even by their minds, but by their reality boxes, and which, if efficient enough, are operating on highly protective automatic.

116

It is thus of interest to consider how reality boxes might be structured or formatted so as to achieve whatever efficiency they do.

For starters, STRUCTURE is not just a building of some kind, as many think, but is best generically defined as: "something made up of interdependent parts in a definite manner of construction and in a definite pattern of organization."

The term DEFINITE refers to "having distinct or certain limits that are clear, constant, unmistakable and precise."

Generally speaking, the "interdependent parts" of a reality box can be thought of as FRAMES OF REFERENCE.

FRAME is defined as: "something composed of parts fitted together and united; the constructional system that gives shape or strength."

FRAME OF REFERENCE is defined as: "a set of systems (as of facts or ideas) serving to orient or give particular meaning."

117

Here is the first and perhaps foremost problem when considering how and why reality boxes are structured.

For, if reality boxes are made up of frames of reference, we find that those can be made up not only of facts, but also of IDEAS – as John Locke indicated some centuries ago.

The term IDEA has several definitions, of course, but two of them have relevance to reality boxes – "a formulated thought or opinion" and "whatever is known or supposed regarding something."

The term TO SUPPOSE really leads this discussion into deep waters, for it is taken from the Latin term meaning "substitution."

In English, however, it is given a slightly more elegant definition as "to lay down tentatively as a hypothesis or assumption." In common human experiencing, however, "assumption" is also given a slang definition (yes, you got it already) as "the mother of all ups."

118

From all of this, reality boxes seem to be made up of frames of reference fitted together and united into a constructional system that gives shape or strength, the whole of which is considered clear, constant, unmistakable and precise.

However, frames of reference can include not only facts, but also ideas that serve to orient the constructional system and give it meaning.

Ideas are composed of formulated thought or opinion, and whatever is known or supposed regarding something.

Reality boxes therefore can include suppositions, hypotheses, and assumptions, which can act as substitutions, i.e., something put in place of something else, whether unintentionally or intentionally.

As can be discovered quite easily, substitutions can include misapprehensions, illusions, and even hallucinations.

And, as has already been discussed, reality boxes can incorporate information and knowledge vacuums, and some might have black holes in consciousness composed of who knows what.

Now, one might think that the whole of all of this is quite wobbly, and therefore unlikely to be made into a STRUCTURE of interdependent parts having a definite pattern of organization that is rigid and impermeable enough to have a self-contained efficiency that is strong enough to keep certain things inside and to keep other things outside of it. Well, think again!

Chapter Twenty

SOME REALITY BOX CHARACTERISTICS

119

THE USUAL approach with respect to considering reality boxes of all kinds is to examine the differences between them. This approach might seem straightforward enough and some headway might be made along these lines.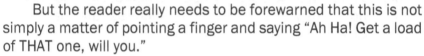
It is, of course, important to compare reality boxes.

But the reader really needs to be forewarned that this is not simply a matter of pointing a finger and saying "Ah Ha! Get a load of THAT one, will you."

The reason this tactic won't serve too well is that it principally consists of one reality box pointing a finger at another one, with the other one pointing back and saying the same thing.

120

There is one basic factor about reality boxes that might be pointed up for what it is worth. It can generally be agreed that they wheel and deal in information packages, and in whatever meanings might be attributed to them.

This same wheeling and dealing is also attributed to the mind, which is why reality boxes are designated as "mental."

One of the purposes in researching the constituents of mind hinges upon the idea that its parts must WORK in certain specific ways in order to function.

Thus arises the assumption within which it is expected that the constituents of the mind will ultimately be identified and methodically itemized, compartmentalized, characterized, and understood in THOSE terms.

Since the mind is thought to be the central control unit of all mental activity, the same assumption is thus extended to include reality boxes and that they have parts that can be itemized and characterized.

121

The basis for this particular assumption is derived from the concept that once it becomes possible to identify all of the interacting constituent parts of something, then it will methodically be understood how it works as a whole, and thereafter methodical applications and better management can be designed for it.

In fact, the whole of the modern sciences rests on this assumption and expectation, and, in certain areas, great and wonderful strides of progress have been achieved.

Even so, there are certain human factors that so far have not responded too well to this methodical approach, and indeed remain notoriously elusive to it – such as the nature of consciousness.

122

To repeat, the idea that reality boxes must have interdependent working parts leads to the expectation that the parts can be identified, compartmentalized, and categorized in order to achieve methodical understanding of them.

A first snag appears quite early in the contexts of this methodical approach. Individuals can accept the idea of reality boxes with respect to others, and can have great entertainment in pointing them out.

However, most individuals do not experience their OWN realities as BOXED. And indeed, on average any intimation that one's own realities are boxed (i.e., rigidly limited) can easily lead toward all too familiar interpersonal stresses and even toward a fracas of some kind.

123

Another snag can be encountered quite early in the study of reality boxes.

This derives from the idea that each individual has a mind, i.e., ONE mind, which is all their own. This important distinction gets lost in studies of THE mind in whose generalizing pursuits individual minds are of interest only in some kind of statistical context.

With respect to individual reality boxes, the idea that there is only one mind leads to the assumption that individuals have only one reality box, which is some kind of subset activity within the one mind.

The snag consists of the following. Individuals in their "normal," everyday working consciousness and social presentation of themselves can usually be seen as having one reality box.

However, when such individuals chance to imbibe one too many glasses of beer or wine, etc., they might, on occasion, suddenly transmute into what was once termed another "visage" of themselves.

This kind of thing is usually explained (away) as only a temporary effect of the drink and weakened self-behavior control.

But what has occurred more precisely is that the drink has brought about some kind of altered state that has distorted if not obliterated the normally presented visage. If the new visage is clear and concise enough, it can be seen as having all the earmarks of another reality box.

124

However, drink is not entirely necessary for reality box switching. Intense emotional trauma can also do it.

Sudden encounters with life threatening danger can sometimes do it, too – during which one's everyday reality box is almost instantly suspended and replaced by a life-survival one. Feats, sometimes referred to as superhuman, occur, the reality of which cannot be accounted for via one's normal, everyday reality box.

It may seem that individuals have only one reality box and that they are confined within its parameters. But then there is the old adage that things are seldom what they seem to be.

The reality box situation might be compared to the famous Chinese Box conundrum. You open the first one, only to find another inside it. Once that is opened, it, too, contains another, and yet another is inside that one, and so forth.

It is difficult to think that one packaged reality box can contain others. But it is possible to think that an inherent consciousness might, and that is what all individuals have BEFORE packaged reality boxes are inserted into it.

Chapter Twenty-One

SOME REALITIES THAT MAY OR MAY NOT BE PRESENT IN THIS OR THAT REALITY BOX

125

AT FIRST TAKE, the heading above might seem a bit stupid for the following reason.

If one accepts the existence, throughout our species, of reality boxes, all formulated on different sets of knowledge, then it is all too obvious that great differences will exist among them, and so examination of the differences will seem a logical kind of enterprise to undertake.

Indeed, this approach characterized the bulk of modernist anthropological and sociological studies during the nineteenth and early twentieth centuries.

Among other subtle results, it led to the idea that DIFFERENCES were of most prime importance with respect to all else.

126

This, in turn, led to the idea that people could best be recognized by their differences, and led to the idea that if one WAS different, then one had a good chance of blipping on everyone's radars.

Put another way, as the artist Andy Warhol did, recognition, and thereby status, and even fame, could come by being different enough to blip on as many socially important radars as possible.

It is easily understood that if differences are great enough, they then have what the modern culture came to identify as "shock value."

In the pre-modern past, such differences were usually eradicated by means often foul in order to preserve a given status quo. But in the scenarios of the modern age, having shock value achieved the positive status of value added because what was shocking enough attracted the widest value-adding attention.

This is best and most easily recognized within the exploitive contexts of the modern arts scene and movie-making factories where shock value was engineered into commercial value added plus.

It was also rather characteristic of the modern approaches to philosophy, and of the modern sciences, especially with respect to the branches of psychology, sociology, and social and political engineering.

If one takes the time to survey the history of these fields, it can be seen that they altogether generated a vast number of theories, the most shocking of which stood a good chance of gaining at least some exposure in major media, and with that, improved possibilities of major funding for testing the theories.

Major media of the modern age did not excuse themselves from this approach after its professionals realized that shock value reporting, including shock value gossip, represented sales value added.

Thus, modern theorists of all types set about focusing on strapping together theories most shocking, and many of them did achieve value added plus, even if, in the end, their theories flopped and disappeared from view.

127

The foregoing, somewhat sardonic, observations are important. One reason is that when individuals want to think of getting outside their box, they are hoping, on average, to achieve some kind of contemporary value-added in terms of increased recognition, increases of status, more money, and other benefits, and, dare it be said, more power.

Those having such hopes need not struggle through this book, but need to be referred to another one, discussed just ahead, that is more in keeping with such aims.

It is not unusual to think that discovering what is in reality boxes will add to one's knowledge about them.

This is especially the case with respect to the reality boxes of those who have become successful in some way, particularly with regard to one's betters, as it used to be put, and especially to those who have achieved modicums of wealth, influence, power, and status, etc.

After all, finding out how others tic does suggest that by emulating them one might learn to tic in the same way.

A particularly good example of this kind of effort is found in a book entitled THE 48 LAWS OF POWER by Robert Green and Joost Elffers, published in 1998.

As blurbs on the dust jacket reveal, the book is "a piercing distillation of three thousand years of the history of power" and is "amoral, cunning, ruthless, and instructive" with respect to work, relationships, and street smarts, and to interests involving conquest, self-defense, or simply being an educated spectator."

It is implied that readers might emulate the hundreds of tidbits therein so as to induce more success in their own desires or goals.

128

The book is a fascinating read within its own considerable dimensions. But if it is placed in the contexts of reality boxes, it can take on additional meaning and inspiration, because every item in it represents a reality box of some kind or other, and in that sense the book is quite an eye-opener.

So, this particular book is a must for anyone interested in MORE influence, status, and power of various kinds, and as a broad spectrum of what may or may not be found in this or that reality box.

At the least, it decreases naivety (which is a reality box in its own right), and it saves a lot of open fieldwork and observational time, in that it is a sort of tourist map pointing up what to look for and see.

129

Even if the book is a valuable one, it is rather sparse in discussing at least very important two human consciousness qualities and which are not even mentioned it – which are also found absent in this or that reality box, especially of the blackhole kind.

130

These two human qualities are ETHICS and COMPASSION.

131

Perhaps these two topics are absent in 48 LAWS OF POWER because they are two of several human qualities that absolutely require actual and alive sense of consciousness of them – whereas amoral, cunning, and ruthless reality boxes can get along quite well without entanglements of too much consciousness, or even too much conscience.

If nothing else, 48 LAWS OF POWER establishes that amoral, cunning, and ruthless reality boxes have more or less dominated throughout "three thousand years" of history, and so this is nothing new.

But this author has lived through seventy years of the twentieth century during which the topics of ethics and compassion were diminished to their wholesale lowest ebb ever, perhaps not within every individual, but at least with respect to modernist intellectual, political, sociological, and scientific strata.

132

If history is consulted, it can be seen that the topic of ETHICS was incorporated into educational programs that endured for about a thousand years in the cultural West. Earlier than that, ethics had long been a central issue in philosophical discourse in antiquity, especially in Greece and China.

In my own collegiate years, such a course was still being

offered, albeit having a real interest in ethics already made one something of a nerd or a social outcast among one's peers. Near the end of the twentieth century, however, one could learn that most educational systems, including some universities, had closed down their ethics courses.

As to COMPASSION, it is difficult to discover any past or present conventional organized educational curricula for it.

Compassion seems to have been left to Eastern and some Western mystics to consider, which they did at some length, although they seemed to have had little real effect elsewhere.

ETHICS is, of course, defined as: "The discipline dealing with what is good and bad with the moral duty and obligation to sponsor the good and diminish the bad."

COMPASSION is defined as: "Sympathetic consciousness of others' distress together with a desire to alleviate it."

133

Both ethics and compassion can be classified under the rubrics of "empathy" and "moral sentiments", both of which have achieved recognition in Donald E. Brown's List of Human Universals, as presented in the Appendix of Steven Pinkers' book, THE BLANK SLATE: THE MODERN DENIAL OF HUMAN NATURE, discussed earlier.

However, the universality of "moral sentiments" is discussed only in relation to the "limited range of." Yes, we got it – and many have known this all along.

As will be discussed ahead, one reason why moral sentiments have a limited range is that they seem somehow to be appended to two other innate faculties, those of empathy and telepathy, and which, if not nurtured, decrease sensitivity to ethics and compassion.

It can be understood why amoral, cunning, and ruthless reality boxes can become alarmed by the nurturing of too much compassion and ethics – and so blank slate enthusiasts exclude such nurturing.

So, with respect to some realities that may or may NOT be present in this or that reality box, there appear to be two principal types of reality boxes: those containing at least some modicum of ethics and compassion realities, and those that contain little or nothing of them.

Chapter Twenty-Two

AMORAL, CUNNING, AND RUTHLESS REALITY BOXES

134

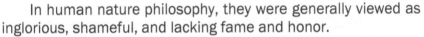

AMORAL, CUNNING, AND RUTHLESS realities have of course existed for a long time, so much so that they were included as attributes in the warp and weave of what used to be philosophically called the total "fabric of human nature."

In human nature philosophy, they were generally viewed as inglorious, shameful, and lacking fame and honor.

As a result, proper efforts at philosophical study and theorizing usually managed to swim around them in order to erect some kind of seamless picture of human nature's higher and more glorious attributes. And so, the inglorious attributes existed without achieving something akin to a philosophical foundation.

HISTORICAL TIDBIT. A political treatise written by Niccolò Machiavelli (1469-1527), the Italian author and statesman, came into print in 1532, entitled THE PRINCE. It described methods whereby a prince may gain and maintain his power. This book became a runaway best seller from the start, is still in continuous print today, and is required reading in some universities.

From this book is derived MACHIAVELLIANISM, a term quickly inducted, in about 1570, into the English language, is described as consisting of "the view that politics is amoral and that any means however unscrupulous, and irrespective of morality, can justifiably be used in achieving political power."

135

In its formal sense, Machiavellianism is considered as a "political theory." But since such theories can be vague in the extreme, they are given more substance if they are thought of as having real philosophical contexts. Indeed, political parties everywhere seldom advertise themselves as having merely a theoretical basis.

Thus, a theoretical basis can, by Machiavellian cunning, be transmuted into something akin to a legitimate philosophical realism, and the coast is then clear with respect to justifying unscrupulous methodologies.

However, a study of Machiavellian realities shows that they only work in the presence of great mental clumps of naivety and/or stupidity on the parts of many others, and which is probably why such clumps are thought to be such a valuable resource and should somehow be maintained as such.

136

HISTORICAL TIDBIT. Now, one thing might not have anything to do with another. But some fifty years after the introduction of the Machiavellian scenario, it transpired, in about 1581, that the venerable Greek term ETHIKOS was dusted off, and inducted into English with the meaning of "relating to morals."

It was reformulated, in about 1607, as the adjective ETHICAL, which, in its earliest definition, referred to "of or pertaining to morality or the science of ethics."

Prior to these particular developments, which, to be sure, are English nuances given to ETHIKOS, morals were generally thought of as "Excellence of character or disposition, as distinguished from intellectual virtue," and increasing an awareness of same via "The moral teaching or practical lesson of a fiction or fable, sometimes of a real occurrence."

137

It may need to be pointed up that social structures ultimately need to depend on the actual excellence of character or disposition of at least some important few.

Otherwise, the whole might fall victim to supposed "intellectual virtues" that may end up being not exactly what they are cracked up to be – and lest, thereby, the structure itself might fall into moral, to say nothing of economic, bankruptcy.

138

While it is, admittedly, somewhat difficult to study and recognize how ETHIKOS was utilized a thousand years ago, one factor about it can emerge. Whatever could contribute to excellence of character or disposition did not, shall we think, achieve the social legitimacy in ways that the introduction of Machiavellianism did.

What IS the larger case, however, is that activities approximating the Machiavellian scenario have been going on, within all social scenarios, since Day One. But they had seldom been granted status equal with, or more important and interesting than, excellence of character and disposition.

There is, of course, much to argue about here, principally because much is entirely relative to this or that reality box. Even so, distinctions can be made between reality boxes demonstrating excellence of character and disposition and reality boxes demonstrating relative or total absence of same.

139

CONTINUING HISTORICAL TIDBIT. After about 1600, definitions of ETHICS and MORALS began to flower in ways that were thought meaningful, at least up to about 1900. To wit: "Of or pertaining to character or disposition as good or bad, pertaining to the distinction between right and wrong, or good or evil, in relation to the actions, volitions, or character of responsible beings."

It could be thought something along these lines would be incorporated into the reality-box overviews of modern sociology, and that that field, as important as it became, must have had some serious historical antecedents.

However, that field of study was commenced only in 1843,

when its original reality-box definition WAS closely connected to the substance of ethics, to wit, "The science or study of the origin, history, and constitution of human society, and which is to constitute a new science, to be called Social Ethics - Sociology."

As of about 1967 or earlier, the principal reality-box definition of that field had undergone revisions – so as to exclude the concept of social ethics. Sociology had become "The science of society, social institutions and social relationships; specifically, the systematic study of the development, structure, and function of human groups conceived as processes of interaction or as organized patterns of human behavior."

140

The perceptive eye might observe that the contexts of Social Ethics had, between 1843 and 1967, somehow been excluded from the more contemporary definition – which implies that an important reality-box shift had taken place.

Why this shift occurred is discussed by Irving Louis Horowitz, himself a distinguished sociologist at Rutgers University, in his 1993 book entitled THE DECOMPOSITION OF SOCIOLOGY.

"Sociology," he writes, "has changed from a central discipline of the social sciences to an ideological outpost of political extremism. As a result, the field is in crisis. Some departments have been shut down, others cut back; research programs have dried up, and the growth of student enrollment either has been curbed or has atrophied."

In other words, the drift in sociology away from the reality box of social ethics to, of all things, "political extremism" is also the drift from social ethics to the reality boxes of Machiavellianism within which ethics, or compassion for that matter, does not play a very large role.

PART FIVE

GETTING OUT OF
THE BOX?

Chapter Twenty-Three

ESCAPING LIMITATIONS TO CONSCIOUSNESS

141

AT THIS POINT, it might be obvious that thinking outside the box, or getting outside of one, is not altogether straightforward. Succeeding at this kind of project would actually entail getting outside of whatever limitations to thinking, awareness, and consciousness that have become set and fixed in one's reality box.

Something about this seems to depend on two factors: how one thinks of oneself in the first place; and how one is thought of by others – which is to say, by one's group and peers, etc. The latter is perhaps even more important, in that once one is pegged by others this way or that, others tend to be resistive to changes one might undergo.

142

In the pre-modern past, most social groupings were, on average, built upon systems that were stratified into rigid classes, between which no upward mobility was possible. These systems were founded upon the concept of clans and bloodlines. The parameters of these were protected, and any changes therein were closely guarded at both the highest and lowest strata.

In this sense, discrete individuality did not exist, and one thought of oneself as a part of whatever clan or bloodline they had been born into. Although vestiges of this reality box still exist here and there, today people are thought of as discrete individuals, at least on the surfaces of social interaction.

Indeed, the principles and contexts of individualism are so familiar worldwide that it may seem they have been present throughout history.

143

HISTORICAL TIDBIT. It is surprising to discover that the theory and doctrine of individualism came into existence only about 150 years ago, and, as it turned out, they are purely an invention from within the freedom-seeking principles of the United States.

In the early 1830s, the French politician and writer, Alexis de Tocqueville (1805-1859), came on a government mission to the United States to undertake observations about American penal systems. It transpired that he exceeded that particular goal of his mission, and proceeded to observe everything else American, too. This resulted in his famous book, in four volumes, entitled DEMOCRACY IN AMERICA.

It was in those volumes that the various elements of individualism took on concrete shape, and were ultimately merged into the doctrine. De Tocqueville was convinced that (the reality boxes of) political democracy and social equality would, inevitably, replace (the reality boxes of) aristocratic institutions of Europe, and that much could be learned from the successes and failures of American attempts to have both liberty and equality.

144

The elements of what became realized as INDIVIDUALISM had never been codified before. But these were soon ironed out and defined as:

1) A doctrine that the interests of the individual are or ought to be ethically paramount;
2) Conduct guided by such a doctrine;
3) Self-centered feeling or conduct as a principle;
4) A mode of life in which the individual pursues his own ends, and follows out his own ideas;
5) Free and independent action or thought.

145

Back at the startup of this doctrine in the latter decades of the nineteenth century, the idea that ANYONE and EVERYONE could have equal equality was astonishing. At the best, it was generally considered by the rest of the world, and even by many Americans, as ridiculously vulgar, unbelievably parvenu, and clearly pretentious.

At its worst, it was thought totally without well-founded logic and hence destructive of traditional class systems that kept things in order and in an appropriate place.

In retrospect, many facets of individualism have turned out quite nicely and productively, and many have benefited thereby.

If the whole of this is converted into reality box contexts, it can be seen that the newly emerging American reality box of individualism impacted rather heavily on other older social reality boxes, and ultimately did so throughout the world. Indeed, the nineteenth and twentieth centuries have sometimes been referred to as the American ones.

146

But there is still one nagging facet. This is partly reflected in the now familiar but sardonic observation that "some remain more equal than others."

What also nags has to do with the question of who is to have this or that status among all those who, under the provisos of the theory or doctrine of individualism, are equal.

While the dissemination of democratic individualism brought down the older social formats of rigid class systems (although reality boxes of some of these are still on-going here and there), the situation with respect to who is to have status among all of the equal remains somewhat up in the air.

Some efforts have been made to examine this situation, but which, if gone into deeply enough, mostly reveals that just beneath the surface of ethical social individualism there are many social reality boxes throughout the world that are entirely resistant to it.

Therefore, while one can conceptualize oneself as a discrete individual, which is entirely a good thing, on average one must nevertheless interact with social vectors that are resistant to this, especially concerning matters of status.

Most already realize this, of course, but it is enlightening to read a rather revealing up-to-date book that focuses on the matter.

SNOBBERY: THE AMERICAN VERSION, by Joseph Epstein published in 2002, is a humorous page-turner. But one should not be too much fooled by the title, for its pages reveal some significant reality box status issues within which one's sense of self as an individual can undergo challenge.

147

The foregoing has been a rather long-winded way of getting into the substance of this section, which has to do with (1) whom, at the individual level wants to get out of their reality box, versus (2) those who don't want anything of the kind to happen, at least not too much so.

Here is a situation within the contexts of individualism that has never quite made its way onto anyone's radar screen. In any event, it can be at least somewhat understood that those who have achieved, by one way or another, wealth, influence, status, and various kinds of social powers, probably can see little reason to get out of THEIR boxes.

For that matter, the same can probably see little reason that others should get out of their boxes, or too many at least. Indeed, too much along these lines would soon lead at least to nervous imbalances among the accepted balances of reality boxes, and which balances anyway are usually fragile enough.

In any event, the substance of this section has been to point up that if one wants to think and get outside of their box, they will soon encounter at least a few others that might not want such a thing to occur. So, to repeat, getting outside of one's box is not at all a straightforward issue.

Chapter Twenty-Four

THE ADVENT OF REALITY BOX AWARENESS

148

THE CONCEPT of getting out of the box is now rather familiar and in parlance everywhere, and so it might seem that it has been with us for a very long time.

However, as already mentioned, the phrase REALITY BOX as a frame of reference did not make its appearance until sometime in the late 1960s or early 1970s. It is still being used in a slang sense, and has not yet been accepted as being representative of anything that can claim official importance. Therefore, those who study origins of ideas might say that reality box is a very young frame of reference, yet only in its infancy, so to speak.

But those who study such origins realize that ideas are usually foreshadowed in one way or another, and that it is the foreshadowing that ultimately requires a neologism via which the substance behind it can achieve its own identity and special frame of reference.

149

Prior to World War II, such foreshadowing is nowhere to be recognized as such, largely, it seems, because REAL still meant REAL, and versions here and there of what was thought to constitute reality had not yet achieved the status of being thought of as representative of real reality.

Instead, via some kind of philosophical tolerance, the versions were viewed, for example, as individual or group thinking, some of which was not exclusively housed in real reality - or as similarities or differences in psychological orientation resulting in individual or group mindsets.

It was generally agreed that just because minds were psychologically set in this or that way did not automatically imply that the sets were altogether representative of real reality, or even in touch with it.

150

However, the advent and culmination of World War II, especially because the culmination did not result in peace, but in the Bomb (atomic and nuclear) which clearly implied the existence of certain real realities that few, if any, humans had any intelligent cognizance or consciousness of.

That realities, especially extravagantly ominous ones such as planet-wide destruction, could exist so far outside any human knowledge of reality ended up altogether bringing into question the authenticity of ANY human perception of the REAL.

151

This seems, at least in part, to have inspired, here and there, the increasingly collective double notion that human perceptions of reality could constitute pseudo-ideas of real reality – and which pseudo-ideas resulted in their own reality depending on what resulted from them.

In this sense, real reality segued over to include, say, optional "realities" that just about anyone could get up and dress their thinking and consciousness with.

Of course, it blurred the margins between what thereto had been thought of as real reality and versions of it, the latter of which now began to have their own reality status – not because they were really real in their own essence, but because really real results could download from them.

152

One of the really real results of World War II was its mind-numbing body count throughout the world, which, of course, places the affairs of that dismal war not principally in some kind of consciousness, but rather into the contexts of black holes in it.

Although available statistics put the count somewhere in the many millions, additional statistics have not been made available, and, in any event, many just vanished so as to have never been statistically accounted for.

The actual body count might have included almost one-sixth of the world's population back then, which was about 2.5 billion.

The possible extent of this body count took a back seat to the ominous threat of wholesale nuclear destruction. Even so, here and there some few began to wonder what kind of CONSCIOUSNESS could have brought it about – this, obviously a very pregnant question.

It was those wonderings that clearly foreshadow a dawning of what ultimately became dubbed as reality box awareness.

Chapter Twenty-Five

ACCESSING THE PANORAMA OF HUMAN REALITY BOXES

153

"ACCESSING" IS a term in computer lingo meaning "getting into," which, in turn, is slang for "connecting up with."

The workings of the two phrases are closely linked to activities regarding finding, locating, or discovering what is to be gotten into or connected up with.

What is involved, on average, with the LINKING activities (if they DO take place) is that they can be chancy, fortuitous, haphazard, random, or contingent, etc. Additionally, if the linking activities DO NOT take place, one is left somewhat at sea.

154

But with respect to ACCESSING in Computerland, none of this is the case – because computers will either access or advise FILE NOT FOUND.

FILE is, of course, an information package that has been written into memory components of the computer's workings, while something depends on how big those memory components are since this determines how many files can be stored in them.

ACCESSING is therefore relevant to projects involving finding, locating, or discovering information packages about reality boxes, since each of them can be thought of as a self-contained computer with reality-box memory storage files against which other reality boxes can be recognized or not.

Admittedly, this may be taking the computer analogy a bit too far. But even so, reality boxes can recognize only what is already filed in and fits with their memory, and are quite infamous for not recognizing other kinds of reality boxes as such.

Indeed, there is some justification in observing that reality boxes often respond to others as if the others are viruses, the introduction of which will distort and destabilize their own working formats.

155

So here is one possible reason why those wanting to get out of the box might have such a difficult time doing so.

As has been referred to earlier, it is quite apparent that reality boxes seldom realize themselves merely as one, and especially as one that has, well, particular reality frames of reference, or, as it might be put, reality limits consistent with those frames of reference.

After all, erecting reality limits seems to be one of the major functions of reality box software programming in the first place. But this ends up meaning that reality boxes see what they do see, and what they do see IS the extent of reality for THEM, which is then taken as REAL reality.

156

Since the concept of reality boxes has come about rather recently, many reality boxes have not yet achieved too much memory storage about the concept, and this would perhaps mean that few, if any, FILES about the actuality of the concept have been written into a reality box memory category.

In a way, this is perfectly logical, in that many reality boxes do not remember, thus see, that they ARE reality boxes only.

And in THAT sense, they cannot SEE that they are merely one reality box in what is otherwise a vast panorama of them.

157

The theme of getting outside the box (individual, group, etc.), of course, refers to getting outside of the limits of the box, which implies that in so doing one will thereby become enabled to think and act outside of the former limits.

But there is now a question to be considered. If one gets outside, what, then, does one get into? Well, one obvious answer is that one emerges into the vast panorama of other reality boxes.

And it is THIS that implies that unless one becomes at least some kind of a virtuoso regarding reality box information packages, what happens AFTER getting outside may remain, shall we say, somewhat confusing.

158

Considering the immediate foregoing, it may be that bringing reality box information packages into one's inside, so as to increase the size and dimensions of memory storage of them, could be the way to go.

THIS consideration might possibly have shock value, largely because it suggests the opposite of what most might think appropriate. There is the old adage that the more one learns or knows of something, the easier it is to manage.

But this brings up the question as to where information packages about reality boxes, as such, might be linked up with.

Chapter Twenty-Six

SEARCHING FOR INFORMATION PACKAGES DESCRIPTIVE OF REALITY BOXES

159

ABOUT TWENTY-FIVE years ago, a famous editor of books told me what was wrong with my own literary efforts.

"In the texts of your writings," she said, "you identify books that MUST be read if readers should want to know more about what you are talking about. This is an unspoken no-no in the publishing business for two reasons. Publishers are in business to sell YOUR book, not books of others, especially if they are books from other publishers. Also, readers want to end up feeling that they have been fully informed, at least in a brief or condensed way, of everything they need to know about what you are writing about. This is what makes it seem worthwhile to buy your book, and to have made the reading of it seem rewarding and satisfying. If you say there is more elsewhere, then readers do not feel as fulfilled."

There is some logic to this, at least from a competitive sales point of view, and especially within an information glut.

Indeed, a book IS always something of a condensed information package, and the more condensed the better, as evidenced, for example, by the enormous sales of Reader's Digest, and the more recent books for idiots and dummies.

Even bibliographies in books are not actually meant to

suggest what others SHOULD read. Rather, they are lists of what the author has (perhaps too selectively) read, examined, judged, and condensed so as to figure somewhere within the book itself.

160

The foregoing might seem a slight digression from the central themes of this book. But the purpose is point up that there are some topics that are, as it is said, larger than life, and thus larger than books that condense information into this or that information package.

One of those topics is comprised of the panorama of human reality boxes, which is hugely extensive to say the least of it. Any idea that the manifold elements of that panorama can be CONDENSED into a given book, even into this one, is clearly something of an intellectual artifice or illusion more convenient to sales or ego management than anything else.

As it is, though, those who take an interest in the contexts of reality boxes will want to try to find out an expansive more, rather than a condensed less, about them - and, as discussed earlier, this implies the desirability of linking into, or accessing, as many information packages about them as possible.

161

Such information packages have actually proliferated everywhere, but not specifically under the file heading of reality boxes – which, as we know, is a relatively new frame of reference.

For example, by far the biggest resource for reality-box information packages is found in human history itself.

This history is conventionally thought of as the line-up of events, happenings, changes, and individual and group movers and shakers as they sequentially took place throughout the centuries – each within their respective socio-environments.

But history is also the line-up of frames of reference that go along with the events, etc. Since the construction of reality boxes seems to begin with the construction of frames of reference, it seems that history can also be retrospectively viewed through the lenses of reality-box research.

162

Of course, history is "remembered" by historians, and so reality-box research is at first at their mercy, largely because versions of history have been filtered, edited, and packaged via the knowledge, attitudes, and, yes, reality boxes of this or that historian.

While conventional histories seek to recover and record events, etc., which are taken as real and factual of and in themselves, such histories often fail in taking notice of certain details that issue more from motivational reality boxes than of the events themselves.

Even so, human history can probably be thought of as chains of interacting reality boxes, out of which and because of which events occur, and within which certain "historical" figures (i.e., individuals and groups) find their memorable place.

And so, from the greater tableau of history, many information packages about reality boxes can be identified. This might not fully explain those reality boxes, but at least it might induce interest about WHAT, for heaven's sake, our predecessors were using as reality boxes during their given times.

History is therefore the first direct resource for reality box study, for the nature of historical reality boxes can be deduced from or because of events that downloaded from them.

Chapter Twenty-Seven

TWO EXAMPLES OF PRECUSORS FORESHADOWING THE EMERGENCE OF REALITY BOX STUDIES

163

THE END of World War II and increasing knowledge of its black-hole-like atrocities, also accompanied by the black hole portents of the Nuclear Age, aroused three kinds of amazing social repercussions that the Progressive Modern Age was unprepared to deal with.

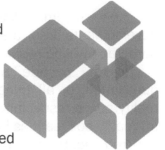

Although the first two repercussions were easily recognizable (because they have been experienced throughout history), it was their dimensions that were surprising: extensive worldwide unrest, and equally extensive loss of faith in leaders of all kinds.

The repercussions of the dawning of the age of potential nuclear destruction were unfamiliar, because it had to do with extensive wondering what human life and consciousness actually MEANT if humans themselves could obliterate both by implementing instruments of massive nuclear holocaust.

164

Elements of this kind of wondering almost certainly evolved into what became collectively known as the Consciousness Movement, and whose social-change effects, and even demands, had evolved into rather serious business during the 1960s.

Although it is commonly thought that the consciousness movement (now somewhat defunct) began in the 1960s, it had some important roots in the late 1940s, and especially during the 1950s.

In that decade, a multitude of writings appeared that questioned, of all things, not only the authenticity of human thinking itself (especially its historical patterns), but also what passed for thinking in an unexamined way.

165

Now, to immediately integrate these particular 1950 developments into the themes of this book, the foregoing paragraph will be rephrased as follows.

In that decade, a multitude of writings appeared that questioned, of all things, not only the authenticity of human reality boxes (especially historical ones), but also what passed for reality-box realities in an unexamined way.

You see, the authors of the 1950 writings did not have the concept of reality boxes at hand but would doubtlessly have seized upon it if it had been available to them.

While such writings were many, three of them stand out with some continuing brilliancy, so anyone today, and into the future, interested in reality box information packages really should study them. They are still in print, and in the early years of their availability each quickly sold more than 20 million copies in English, and many more in other languages.

166

The first of these that might be studied was authored by Eric Hoffer and entitled THE TRUE BELIEVER (1951).

As a major blurb described, "it is an effort, a very laudable one, to examine a bigger picture of the psychology of mass movements and which, as many reviewers noted, is a brilliant and frightening study of the mind [read reality box] of the fanatic, whose personal failings lead him to erect, to join, and to perpetuate a [reality box] cause, any cause, "even at the peril to his life – or yours."

Now, it is really counter-productive to reduce a bigger picture to a smaller-picture thumbnail one-liner, as just above. And so, books attempting to describe or portray a bigger reality picture should be read in their bigger-picture entirety. As it is, this book is not very long, and is written in remarkably concise and fluid narrative, often blunt in impact.

Among other elements discussed, it addresses the appeal of mass movements; desire for change; the role of undesirables in human affairs, including various types of the poor; misfits; the inordinately selfish; minorities; factors promoting self-sacrifice; the deprecation of the Present; fanaticism; unifying agents, such as hatred, imitation, suspicion, and persuasion; men of words; and practical men of action.

As the continuing sales of this book attest, it is a gripping read.

167

If one actually reads the book, one will encounter a facet that most blurbs about it do not pick up on, because most reviewers cast the limelight onto the fanatics.

That facet is this. In his preface, Hoffer utilizes the word "frustrated," the meaning of which is offered up in a footnote, to wit: "The word 'frustrated' is not used in this book as a clinical term. It denotes here people who, for one reason or another, feel that their lives are spoiled or wasted."

And thereby, we can contextually link up Hoffer's book with one of the principal themes in this one – that reality boxes of fanatics (especially of the black-hole kind) can and do spoil or waste the lives of many.

168

A second book from the 1950s that stands out as a reality-box study is entitled THE OUTSIDER (1956), by Colin Wilson, and who, at the time he wrote it, was only 23 years of age.

His book "caused such excitement on both sides of the Atlantic," and especially in England where four printings were sold out within a few weeks of publication.

As one important English reviewer indicated: "Despite his young age, Wilson steps immediately into the ranks of major writers. He has assurance, authority, a mature case of style, considerable facility, learning, and – above all – a theme that is both original and important, which he develops skillfully and persuasively."

TIME magazine, in a prepublication story entitled "Intellectual Thriller," described the theme of the book "as the reason for the excitement it was sure to cause."

So, what was the "theme?" There are many interpretations of what it was. But in retrospect, THE OUTSIDER has a fair claim to being THE founding document of the ever-evolving point of the consciousness movement to date.

Otherwise, it is the most dynamic, bigger-picture line-up of reality boxes ever erected, and into which Wilson weaves, of all things, certain important elements of the strange mind briefly discussed earlier herein.

Indeed, most of Wilson's subsequent books exclusively deal with strange mind phenomena of innate consciousness, albeit under the sobriquet of "the occult."

THE OUTSIDER is a joy to read, especially for those wanting to get out of the box, and, as well, for anyone interested in reality boxes.

In it are discussed numerous themes: the "country of the blind," this referring to conventional societies that are "blind" to anything except conformity with their own internal order; world without values; the question of identity; the romantic outsider; the outsider as visionary; the Great Synthesis; and "breaking the circuit" imposed by various "blind" reality boxes.

This author does not like to "drop names," as it were. But when the man himself once visited me, and I brought up the idea of reality boxes, he confessed the regret he did not have that context at hand when he wrote THE OUTSIDER, and which clearly deals with reality-box situations because of which so many are spoiled and wasted.

Chapter Twenty-Eight

"WHAT MOVES THE WORLD?"

169

AS POINTED UP in the preceding section, numerous sources can be found describing various kinds of reality boxes, but which were written before that frame of reference became available.

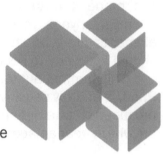

And this author, with hands trembling, will now attempt to discuss yet another one, which is a most superlative example of the reality-box genre viewed retrospectively.

The author of this source was perhaps the most marvelous and most formidable creative thinker to have appeared on the philosophical scene as it was staged during the twentieth century - and who, by being both marvelous and formidable, aroused an entirely monumental ruckus among her somewhat lesser intellectual peers whom she enraged.

170

We are speaking, of course, of the venerable Ayn Rand (1905-1982), a figure so much larger than life, as it is said, that it is difficult to identify any near equivalent personage.

One of the difficulties here is that Rand was clearly a positive creative thinker. The twentieth century did not produce too many of these, because, as some historians have noted, it was the bloodiest, negative-thinking, war-filled century on record both in scope and in worldwide intensity. Wholesale destruction was the name of the major game, and, in its deplorable contexts, positive creative thinking held little meaning or interest.

Indeed, if Rand had not been entirely and awesomely formidable, the chances are very good that her work, and the sum of it, would have fallen into obscurity like so many other creative thinking prospects did.

171

Before continuing, there is one element that needs to be discussed. Rand achieved a tremendous following within which she made it crystal clear that she neither liked, nor would tolerate, anyone messing with her work by introducing odd elements into it, and that anyone attempting anything of the kind should get ready to head for the hills.

This humble author, practically and admittedly a devotee of Rand, is entirely sensitive to this. And so his hands tremble at the prospect of attempting to place the contexts of reality boxes anywhere near adjacent to her work, even in hypothetical theory.

172

There is one small justification for this, and it is found in Rand's own work. She was entirely adamant that if things were not going well, then one should first check one's own "basic premises" before going off halfcocked in blaming others.

The term PREMISE has two relevant definitions: "A proposition antecedently supposed or proved as a basis of argument or inference;" and "To set forth beforehand as introductory or as postulated."

A POSTULATE, as everyone knows, is "a hypothesis advanced as an essential presupposition or premise of a train of reason [or of reasoning]."

The definitions of PREMISE and POSTUATE are nearly identical to the definition of FRAME OF REFERENCE which is given as: "An arbitrary set or system, as of facts or ideas, serving to orient or give particular meaning" – or, as it may as well be pointed up, give particular reality-box frameworks.

173

Thus, there appear to be TWO basic kinds of premises,

postulates, and frames of reference – those based in facts (the Ayn Rand kind), and those based in assumptions, suppositions, presuppositions, and ideas (almost everyone else's kind).

If reality boxes are made up out anything at all, they are certainly constructed BECAUSE of, or in the light of, frames of reference, and hence of premises and postulates as well.

174

Now, not at all wanting to put words into Rand's magnificent and fearsome mouth, it can safely be said, I think anyway, that she was particularly disgusted with "basic" premises mostly or entirely formulated out of suppositions, presuppositions, and factless-based ideas.

Her obvious enthusiasm for spotlighting these in (excruciating) detail unambiguously constitutes the second major theme in her famous (some say infamous) philosophical novel entitled ATLAS SHRUGGED first published in 1957.

The appearance of this book managed to seriously shake up, even enrage, the complacent certitudes of a great many reality boxes everywhere – so much so that the ensuing debates were regularly featured in major media during the following thirty years.

175

So, what is ATLAS SHRUGGED about?

This author acquired the novel either in 1958 or 1959 in its first 1957 paperback edition as a Signet Book, via the New American Library, which was already in its thirtieth (30th) printing.

In that edition, there was a first-page blurb entitled WHAT MOVES THE WORLD, followed by the advisement that the novel was "... the story of a man who said that he would stop the motor of the world – and did."

In order to completely grasp what "the motor of the world" is, one really needs to read the novel, because it is quite difficult, and even unfair, to express it in nutshell form.

However, with apologies as to probable incompetence, the motor of the world consists of creative types – especially of inventors, superlative managers, and clear thinkers of some strength, whose works make the world "go" and "move" – and without which the world would soon retrogress into shambles via those lesser types who cannot make anything go, and who are focused only within their own limited and largely dysfunctional versions of themselves. This is the first major theme of the story.

The second major theme involves those who, with then limited talents and vision, cannot make anything "go," and who are thus second-rate to those who can and do. However, some second-raters desire to achieve influence and power, often of the controlling kind, within what is moving in the world, and over those who are moving it.

In order to achieve such influence and power, subtle ways and means have to come into existence that cause the motor geniuses to work on behalf of the greater whole, and within which the second-raters can achieve influence and power over them and everyone else.

Therewith, Rand has, of course, put her razor-like mind on a very age-old story, the Machiavellian reality-box part of which is seldom exposed or highlighted in what amounts to Rand's brain-surgery detail. More of the novel's plot will not be given here, because there is no point in further revealing the gripping tale, or lead-ups to its remarkable culmination.

One of the bigger negative criticisms, often repeated even today, is that people like the men and women Rand writes about don't really exist.

This is somewhat like speaking through blinders. Indeed, one doesn't really need to read the novel in order to realize they have encountered various kinds of, as it may be put, scumbags and bottom-feeders.

In any event, Rand was not talking about people per se, but about various reality boxes that can clearly be identified.

176

ATLAS SHRUGGED runs over a thousand pages, which gave Rand plenty of room to extensively expound on truculent, delicious, most subtle, and most invisible, reality-box details of all kinds.

It is worth mentioning that the torment and furor that followed the publication of ATLAS SHRUGGED would not have come into existence unless she was hitting some really sensitive reality boxes details squarely on the head.

For more book sources unknowingly discussing reality boxes, please see Suggested Reading provided at the end of this book.

PART SIX

THE CRAFT OF KEEPING PEOPLE IN THEIR REALITY BOXES

Chapter Twenty-Nine

REALITY BOX – A "MIND" WITHIN THE MIND?

177

THIS AUTHOR has had the very welcome opportunity of discussing – with a large number of individuals, famous, notable, or otherwise – the matter of getting outside the box.

From such interchanges, it has become clear that although many desire getting out of their boxes, they are, in general, reluctant and even resistant with respect to examining how they got into their boxes in the first place, and what it is that keeps them therein.

This is at least slightly illogical, for if one wants to get outside of a jail, one has to acknowledge and deal with whatever is preventing one from getting outside of it.

178

In the light of this kind of situation, about forty years ago I chanced to discover a tattered copy of a book entitled PRISONS OF THE MIND published near the turn of the century. I would like to refer to it in detail, but some idiot lifted it from my library, and I've never been successful in replacing it.

In any event, the title is suggestive and clear enough for the purposes of this book, for if one wants to get outside the box, one is, in essence, desiring to escape from some kind of prison in one's mind.

As discussed earlier, a little over 300 years ago, the English empiricist, John Locke, sponsored a number of concepts that were novel during his time – and which soon figured in the tenuous realms of philosophical discourse.

Much beyond those realms, however, Locke's concepts still seem to be novel in that no one seems to have paid much PRACTICAL attention to them ever since.

179

To remind, Locke held that although we do have faculties and powers of thinking and reasoning, we nevertheless use them to erect ideas about reality, we derive our understanding as filtered through the ideas rather than through a direct connection to reality itself.

He also pointed up that ideas through which reality is filtered can contain "phantasm and notions," and with "whatever else the mind can employ in thinking," such as, perhaps, illusion, imagination, incorrect "facts," and even no facts at all.

180

Without wanting to put words into Locke's mouth, the result of this idea-making obviously has to do with reality-box making, examples of which are made up of this and that, and whatever else is at hand.

The venerable Ayn Rand was certainly aware of something akin to this, and there can be little doubt that she, the ultimate philosopher she was, had studied the works of all major philosophers, including those of John Locke.

It is entirely credible that ideas can serve as "basic postulates," which is to say, as basic frames of reference, and so Rand advised that if things were not going one's way, then one should first check the validity of one's own basic postulates – and from which whatever passes for understanding is derived.

This is almost the same as saying that one should check the validity of one's basic frames of reference, upon which, and because of which, one's reality boxes come into existence. In the contexts of this book, doing so would help in restructuring, as it were, one's reality box, and in that sense, permit escape from a less functional former one.

181

It turns out, dare it be said, that there is a subtle glitch in checking out of basic postulates and basic frames of reference.

The glitch is this. Although people, in all walks of life, can often identify such in others, it is devastatingly difficult to identify one's own. Attempting to do so can occasion reality-box tremors, even earthquakes, and temporary loss-of-reality-box certainty.

This is one possible reason why people, encountering something for which their reality boxes possess no frames of reference, want first to shoot it, and then talk about it later, if at all.

One possible reason for the agonizing difficulty of self-identifying one's own basic frames of reference is that they may have been mostly acquired or set up in childhood – and since then have subsided into that area of mind ambiguously referred to as the subconscious in whose murky depths they have been working on non-conscious automatic ever since.

182

The purpose of the forgoing discussion has been to point up a very interesting wonderment.

If one accepts the existence of various kinds of reality boxes, then it is at least somewhat logical to think that they are in the mind, products of the mind, but may not be the mind itself.

This is almost the same as saying that reality boxes are created, or erected, or set up in the mind that can accommodate such going's on, but that the mind itself has to be bigger than the constructed reality boxes.

For emphasis, it is possible to consider that the architecture of the innate mind is not exactly the same as the architecture of this or that reality box formulated, or fomented, within it.

The evidence is actually quite good, for it is generally thought that infants born are not already equipped with the reality boxes later inserted into them via socio-environmental programming, etc.

But if so, then this is the same as saying that mind and

reality boxes are not the same thing, and that reality boxes are merely artifacts introduced into the innate mind that is amenable to such introductions.

183

If THIS were the case, then it is possible to think that a number of fresh infants could be extracted from this or that Earth socio-environmental culture, and transported, say, to the planet Mars, after which they would develop reality-box ideas appropriate to the exigencies of life on that Red Planet. Their innate minds would, of course, be equally amenable to such.

184

In earlier pages of this book, a nutshell review was presented of how psychology was historically conceptualized. In one of its earlier stages, psychology was conceptualized as the study of the mind, but later, principally during the twentieth century, ended up being conceptualized as the study of human behavior.

But here one certainly might ask: the behavior of WHAT exactly?

Well, human behavior, overall, is clearly not all of one piece, context, constituency, dynamism, or even of similar minimal understanding.

While certain elements of the innate mind COULD descend and manifest in some kind of behavior, it is more certainly the case that behavior descends out of this or that reality-box constructs whatever each of those may or may not consist of.

185

One of the direct implications of this line of consideration is that psychologists, behavioral psychologists anyway, were not studying behavior of the human mind, but merely whatever behavior downloaded from this or that reality box.

There is even a very telling and open clue with respect to this. It consists of the broadly accepted principal goal of psychotherapy and of psychoanalysis – to return the individual undergoing such therapy or analysis to a norm more in keeping with the desirable and conventional realities and functions within it.

Well! Over time, so-called conventional realities certainly come and go, shift, change, fall, and disappear, and which, anyway, are different in different socio-environmental frameworks.

It is therefore possible to think that although the innate human mind is something of a species permanent feature, changing conventional realities are not permanent.

Indeed, it seems that conventional realities are glued together by little more than groupings of social reality boxes that achieve, for one reason or another, mutual influence and social power, but only for the time allotted to them.

186

Meanwhile, back at the ranch of the INNATE mind (which everyone has a copy of), efforts and struggles to readjust, remodel, or get out of one's reality box (so as to achieve improved benefits thereby), might seem just a tad silly within the scope of the larger innate mind itself – as many historical and contemporary Eastern mystics have pointed up.

187

In any event, it could turn out that whatever basic postulates or basic frames of reference that structurally support this or that reality box may not be as important as those MISSING from them in the first place.

One such missing piece involves the idea, much mistaken, that one's reality box IS one's mind, rather than just an artifact in it. As it is traditionally said, this is almost the same as putting the cart before the horse and expecting anything to happen.

Another frame of reference that might be missing is that one actually HAS an innate mind, as well as the reality boxes that are but artifacts in it.

Yet another frame of reference that might be absent is that one has innate formats of consciousness, some of which are being used, but a greater portion of which are laying around in latent states awaiting arousal.

With respect to this, the reader might return to the section herein entitled Exceptional Human Experience, and even summon up a modicum of motivation to survey Rhea White's website in this regard.

188

Now, herewith a two-part question might be considered: (1) Is it easier to identify one's usually submerged basic frames of reference; or (2) to seek to identify or locate formats of consciousness one innately has, but is not aware of?

Any answer to this is, of course, up to each individual and their current reality box formations.

Chapter Thirty

IS IT REALITY BOXES – OR IS IT PACKAGED FORMATS OF AWARENESS-CONSCIOUSNESS?

189

THERE EXISTS an interesting saying, to wit: If you ask a fish to describe its environment, it will point out everything but the water.

There is yet another interesting saying: You can lead a horse, mule, or jackass to water, but you can't make them drink of it.

It could also be said that you can lead specimens of the human species to their collective bigger picture, but all they'll see is the particular edge on which they are standing.

190

As representatives of a profession now somewhat defunct, philosophers of course want to identify, describe, figure out, and address bigger pictures and their issues.

This is perhaps one reason why philosophers are not interested in human experiencing at the individual level, and which interest, if properly egalitarian enough, would have to be extended to include, say, the lower social orders, the uneducated, the non-intellectuals, and, possibly, even outsiders and creative types.

But with respect to the bigger-picture thing, what philosophers might consider as a bigger picture is quite likely to be whatever looms large in a given philosopher's own reality box – each of which apparently does see enough to achieve obstinate philosophic certitude about them.

This suggests that there are at least as many bigger pictures as there have been philosophers. And this suggests, in turn, that you can lead philosophers to other, perhaps more really real big pictures, but you can't make them drink of them – even in a typical barroom scene where "philosophers" tend to proliferate and expound.

191

You can ask a philosopher to describe what's in a bigger picture, and, like the proverbial fish, he/she will describe everything in it, except one thing – the awarenesses that go with it, and without which everything else within it would not be seen, i.e., perceived.

In fact, it is easy enough to prove that all specimens of the human species actually have awarenesses, but they are so commonly and redundantly present that, like the fish's water, they are not seen.

It can also be stipulated that there are different kinds or types of awareness via which different things become revealed, and so it can justifiably be thought that a veritable, or virtual, or motherboard "ocean" of awareness does exist – but which, like the proverbial "water," flows in different ways and different patterns.

192

Although the foregoing might seem only something of a lament, awareness is of such philosophic INVISIBILITY that no entry for it is provided in the authoritative Encyclopedia of Philosophy (1967, 1972).

That Encyclopedia consists of eight volumes listing other kinds of topics thought meaningful to philosophic inquiry over the last two-and-a-half millennia, approximately.

In case the point being made here is missed, it must be thought that if awareness doesn't exist, then, as it were, neither does anything else.

So the actual line-up consists of awareness first, then reality box constructions based on whatever awareness, then philosophic discussions and debates involving what is in the reality boxes.

However, there is a situation that somewhat explains the difficulties involved with all of this.

The Encyclopedia DOES have an entry for CONSCIOUSNESS, and indicates it as: (1) a term occurring in philosophy, psychology, and common speech with a variety of different meanings; and (2) which meanings will be discussed that are relative to the formulation of several recurrent philosophical problems.

The Encyclopedia then commences to identify two general types of consciousness: (1) the SELF-KNOWLEDGE type, i.e., knowledge that a given self is or has become aware of; and (2) the STATES OF CONSCIOUSNESS type, which are identified via the following, and which must be slowly and carefully considered: "Consciousness includes not only awareness of our own states, but [of] these states themselves, whether we have cognizance of them or not."

Well, did you get THAT one? If not, it's of little wonder, for confusions abound within it.

193

The term COGNIZANT has only one definition – i.e., aware, while the term COGNIZANCE has five: apprehension, perception, observing, notice, and surveillance – but none of which can come about in the absence of aware, that is of aware-ness.

The quoted, confused definition above might therefore be rewritten as follows: "Consciousness awareness includes not only conscious awareness of our own states, but conscious awareness of these states themselves, whether we have conscious awareness of them or not."

Now, in either the formal or rewritten definition, all of this qualifies as philosophical gobbledygook – i.e., wordy and generally unintelligible jargon.

But if one persists in sifting through the jargon, it can dawn upon one that what is being said is not as important as what is NOT being said, or what is being avoided.

What is being avoided is the implication that kinds of awareness exist, which individuals, apparently including philosophers, are not aware of.

194

If kinds of awareness exist which individuals are not aware of, it can be theorized that the total kinds of awareness, taken altogether, actually constitute a spectrum or motherboard of awarenesses all of which COULD be actualized. This sounds like a good thing to achieve, doesn't it?

However, anything approaching general acceptance of this would open up a veritable Pandora's Box of all kinds of awarenesses that many would NOT want to be actualized – and which could be one reason why awareness is NOT given its own entry in the Encyclopedia, to say nothing of many kinds of reality boxes which do not relish the idea of other reality boxes achieving more awareness than they have.

Thus, in any conventional sociological sense, an overall principal way to keep people in their reality boxes is to diminish interest in and knowledge of awareness itself.

It stands to reason that individuals cannot really get out of their reality boxes UNLESS they somehow upgrade and expand their awareness potentials, and precisely so with respect to factors of awareness not yet included in the reality boxes they wish to get outside of.

But this is almost the same as observing that most conventional sociological orders are intolerant of the development of too much awareness about awareness, and especially of its potentials and dimensions.

195

The foregoing is especially relevant to the real existence of strange mind awareness potentials, which were discussed earlier. We have only to consider the prospect and implications of developed and actualized TELEPATHIC awareness to get the general drift of what is being avoided along these lines.

196

The term FORMAT is defined as "the form, size, and general makeup of something," and "a general plan of organization or arrangement."

It is easy enough to see that reality boxes, in their first essence, are made up of this or that frames of reference.

These, to be at least partially workable, must also achieve some kind of general plan of organization or arrangement.

Whatever results from the plan of organization or arrangement has to do with the form, size, and general makeup, or packaging, of the reality box, which, taken altogether, formats its lesser or greater dimensions, as it might be put.

However, frames of reference depend on achieving at least minimal awareness – hence consciousness – of them, and so it can be thought that reality boxes are actually packaged formats of whatever awarenesses are not only included in, but also excluded from them.

Thus, any getting out of the box actually implies accessing additional, or at least different kinds of awareness that somehow or for some reason have not been incorporated into it – but which can be, and, in fact, if this "can be" were not possible, then no one could ever get outside of their reality boxes.

Chapter Thirty-One

THE DISPOSING OF THE STRANGE MIND

197

IF ONE reads history, but does so without a working knowledge of Machiavellian strategy or tactics, it then can seem a somewhat straightforward line-up of events that are connected in objective and apparently logical ways.

Of course, history is also about prominent individuals, or about those who became noteworthy enough for various reasons. But these are presented as having historical importance only with respect to the objective contexts of the times and events within which they lived.

When those times and events have receded into history, so have the prominent individuals involved.

Some parts of history, however, do not merely recede into history, but into oblivion, into historical knowledge vacuums and sometimes into black holes.

Many subtle and not-so-subtle things have disappeared in this way, but, as already established, among those things are the objective bodies and lives of those many who became, in one way or another, abject victims of objective historical goings-on.

198

The tricky word in all of this is "objective," which is generally, and superficially, thought to refer to what is physically out there and, in a condition, at least sufficient enough to establish recognizable thing-ness.

The most fundamental working definitions of OBJECTIVE are

given as (1) existing independent of mind; (2) belonging to the sensible world; and, (3) emphasizing or expressing the nature of reality as it is apart from personal reflections or feelings.

So, when history remembers only what is objectively independent of mind, the historical mind disappears from view – with the strange exception that the historical mind lives on in those born anew, while historical objective events do not.

199

Now, as inferred above, history can be read without any familiarity with the strategies of Machiavellianism. But if it is read in the light of that ism, it becomes obvious that such strategies existed long before Machiavelli codified them in his famous book published in 1537.

One of THE most important aspects of Machiavellian strategies and tactics is that they cannot work too well if they are detected as such. In relationship to this detecting, it must be observed that the chief detecting agency is the human mind, especially if it is up to snuff with respect to the intricacies of such detecting.

200

So, in bigger-picture Machiavellian scheme of things, it transpires that the mind must be disposed of, with special emphasis on its detecting components.

There are two traditional methods for achieve something like this – to keep people, in general, as stupid and illiterate as possible, and, if that doesn't work, to keep their minds fixated on the objective nature of reality as it is apart from minds.

The latter method works quite well, even among the not-so-stupid and the literate. The principal reason is that various systems of LOGIC can be set up, or discovered, among objective realities and things that are, so to speak, interacting with each other in ways that are logical within the interacting.

Two of the principal, and perhaps most important, definitions of LOGIC are given as (1) interrelation or sequence of facts or events when seen as inevitable or predictable; and (2) something that forces a decision apart from or in opposition to reason.

The latter definition implies that logic and reason are not always compatible, but it is beneficial to Machiavellian activities to ensure that they are always thought of as such, i.e., seen as the same thing. The principal reason for THIS is that those who feel their reasoning is based on logic irrefutable (in their own reality boxes, anyway) become easy victims for Machiavellian strategies and tactics.

201

As already pointed up, Machiavellian reality-box activities cannot succeed too well unless the detecting components of mind are disposed of in some wholesale manner. And so arises the question of what those components are.

The first and most familiar of these is deduction, or deducing, the principal definition of which is given as "the deriving of a conclusion by reason, specifically, inferences in which the conclusion follows necessarily from the premises," i.e., from the reality-box frames of reference being utilized.

In the contexts of Machiavellian activities, dealing with the deducing components of mind is merely a piece of cake. Introducing a few subtle mental viruses, or a little mind F-word, will easily distort this or that information package, and Machiavellians can thus get on with it.

202

But this is not the case with the detecting components referred to as intuition, generally defined as "the power or faculty of attaining to direct knowledge or cognition without rational thought and inference."

Via this definition, the intuition components of mind are several cuts above the deducing ones.

It can also be observed that the intuition components must somehow be external to reality boxes, because the intuition components do not seem to operate only with respect to the limits of given reality-boxes.

And the resulting "direct knowledge and cognition" usually exceeds frames of reference that serve as foundations for reality-box "rational thought and inference." This is one reason why intuition is referred to as being irrational, and thus not amenable to rational explanation.

203

Dealing with the intuition components, which are, to be sure, components of the strange mind, is NOT a Machiavellian piece of cake. Like inspiration and insight, two other detecting components of the strange mind, intuition arrives when it does, but arrives from who knows where, and who knows why.

These detecting components are not OBJECTIVE, i.e., outside and independent of mind, but have the temerity of emerging from mind itself – or at least from a part of the motherboard of consciousness that apparently does not altogether permit itself to be conditioned into abject conformity with objective realities of the sensible world that are apart from mind.

Furthermore, these detecting components apparently have their own logic, and so their activities are not logical, i.e., not predictable within the contexts of objective realities which are. Since Machiavellian strategists and tacticians can make headway only within contexts that remain relatively predictable with respect to others, they can be rather irritated by the mind-consciousness parts that do not.

This is almost the same as saying that Machiavellians have no defenses against strange-mind functions such as intuition, insight, or telepathy for that matter.

204

So, some descriptive terms have come into existence for such irritating parts of mind-consciousness, the kindest of which is "strange mind," and whose contexts and activities must be disposed of in any Machiavellian way possible.

Indeed, during the last two millennia at least, wherever strange-mind activities got underway in any important sociological sense, it can be shown that conventional societies responded negatively to them, even if justified or covered up by other propaganda.

As to what the disposal might consist of, well, even the proverbial dummies realize what can happen if the equally proverbial Machiavellian games are upset or thwarted. The most contemporary term for this seems to be "whacked," in one way or another. Some predecessor references were crucifixion, immolation at the stake, other persecutions, and, as one of the larger black holes in consciousness, genocide.

So, although strange mind potentials exist within the fuller spectrum of consciousness of our species, and hence in all individuals, there has always been some kind of sociological objection involved.

An excellent review of both of these aspects is found in a most impressive study of what is involved, authored by Brian Inglis under the title of NATURAL AND SUPERNATURAL: A HISTORY OF THE PARANORMAL FROM EARLIEST TIMES TO 1914, first published in 1977. This book is a gripping read for those interested in its substance, and the often shocking events reported in it.

Chapter Thirty-Two

THE DISPOSAL OF TELEPATHY

205

WHAT IS today thought of as telepathy is almost certainly a capacity belonging to the strange-mind part of mind, which is basically defined, in modern parapsychology, as "empathy over or across distance," or as "mind-to-mind".

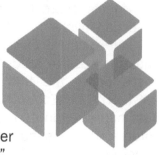

In common parlance, it is better and more correctly known as mind READING (or psyching out someone's mental whatever). In that sense, if one thinks that the idea of mind reading does not irritate controllers of Machiavellian projects, one should make haste to do a little reality-box retooling.

206

HISTORICAL TIDBIT. One of the earlier, and important, founding concepts of telepathy was enunciated by Paracelsus (1493?-1541), the famous (some said infamous) Swiss physician, chemist, and alchemist, whose egotism and contempt for traditional theories earned him the enmity of his learned contemporaries. Even so, he gained wide popularity among the people and had great influence on his own and succeeding generations.

One possible contributing factor for the enmity may have gotten underway when Paracelsus indicated that "a man may know what another man thinks at a distance of 100 miles or more." Now, however he was viewed, Paracelsus was a man intent on collecting and collating factual evidence, but whatever his evidence about this 100-mile thing seems to have been lost.

In any event, the term TELEPATHY did not exist during Paracelsus' time. It is of rather recent vintage, being coined only in 1882. Before that, the same was thought of as neuro-empathy, as thought-transference, earlier as thought-reading, again earlier as RAPPORT – i.e., "relation marked by harmony, conformity, accord, or affinity."

These four rather pleasant nuances still cling to ideas about telepathy, so much so that many think telepathy is not possible without them.

207

As might at least be imagined, achieved Machiavellian enthusiasts and manipulators are NOT that dumb, and they were not that dumb either circa, say, 1520 when Paracelsus was proceeding upwards into his remarkable ascendancy.

It is part and parcel of tested and proven Machiavellians to recognize a threat when they see one. Indeed, if a man might know what another man thinks at a distance of 100 miles, well, THIS, whatever it might be called, is not merely a gnat on a rat's ass.

Rather, it is an invasive threat pure and simple with respect to secrets, to covert plots and plans of any kind, to undisclosed mind control techniques, to hidden purposes of social programming, and to whatever the man 100 miles distant might not want shared with another, no matter how distant he is.

208

If viewed from this perspective, telepathy must somehow be sociologically disposed of, even if it is an innate part of the fuller spectrum of human consciousness.

209

From this collective point of view, and it IS a rather large collective one, the idea telepathy might contain positive potentials for establishing harmony, conformity, accord, and affinity is completely irrelevant and, furthermore, NOT open to negotiation.

Reality Boxes | 150

Additionally, although developed telepathy might help thwart or prevent great human-made calamities brought about by Machiavellian activities and might help reduce the frequency of black holes in human consciousness that suck millions of lives, etc., any and all aspects of telepathy must be disposed of, and in any way possible.

210

There have been many ways to affect this disposal. During the pre-modern past, one way was simply to terminate, on behalf of various justifications, the lives of those who exhibited anything resembling telepathic intuition and insight – especially with respect to women who seem to have more active telepathy than men do.

Even after this kind of "solution" became morally questionable during the early 1800s, telepathy still needed somehow to be disposed of, especially in the case of the modern sciences whose familiar contexts began to be formulated circa 1845.

One of the principal goals of the modern sciences was to submit everything to scientific examination.

However, the early leaders of the scientific community almost unanimously decided to exclude any inquiry into telepathy, and, as well, into anything suggestive of being psychic, i.e., anything of the strange mind aspects of our species.

As everyone realizes, definitions of psychical matters involve "sensitivity to nonphysical or supernatural forces and influences/ and whatever is "immaterial, moral, or spiritual in origin or force.

But there is a so-called "scientific" definition still on record – i.e., "lying outside the sphere of physical science or knowledge." And it was via this definition that scientific examination of "everything" could exclude examination of telepathy, etc.

211

With the advent, outside of the conventional sciences, of organized psychical research in 1882, and of parapsychology during the early 1930s, more subtle means of denying the existence of telepathy was to conduct research and testing of it – the usual results of which either showed that the experiments didn't work, or that the results, if any, were statistically so low as to be sociologically irrelevant.

When this happened, as it often did, the sponsors and other factotums of the conventional sciences were pleased enough to hype the negative results.

The only remaining problem had to do with organized telepathic research that resulted in high statistical relevance and success. It turned out that these could simply be ignored by the conventional sciences, and thus become submerged in the increasingly dusty and apparently useless archives of parapsychology.

212

There is yet another bottom-line way to dispose of telepathy. It involves discouraging and NOT providing any significant funding for research into it. Even parapsychologists, and just about everyone else, lose interest in whatever does not attract funding.

Did you get that? If not, for clarity: No money, no development and enhancement of the telepathy potentials of our species.

PART SEVEN

APPROACHING THE BIGNESS OF HUMAN CONSCIOUSNESS?

Chapter Thirty-Three

MEASURING THE PARAMETERS OF CONSCIOUSNESS

213

IF CONSCIOUSNESS IS bigger than we think, a number of interesting and somewhat complicated questions arise.

Perhaps the first of these hinges on comparing (1) what people do experience of consciousness with (2) the presumed bigger whole of it which they do not experience.

This comparison is difficult to undertake because people are not aware of what they don't experience simply because they have never become aware of it – i.e., one cannot become aware of consciousness aspects they have not become aware of.

The whole of this might at first seem merely as a tumbling play of words. But the fact is that if individuals do not experience awareness of this or that aspect of consciousness, then such aspects simply do not exist for them.

214

But there are two other facts that need to be acknowledged. First, people everywhere, and in all times and situations, have to get along within the contexts of what they have achieved awareness of, and, second, what they have achieved awareness of will be used to define or circumscribe not only what consciousness IS, but what its parameters are or must be.

Obviously, such definitions of consciousness cannot include circumscription of whatever they have not achieved awareness of, and which hence cannot be included in definitions of consciousness.

By far and large, people are not aware of what they not aware of. Furthermore, what they are not aware of is not experienced as an absence or even as a nothing – with the possible exception of that ever-brooding question having to do with becoming at least somewhat aware that there is more to them than they know about.

215

As indicated, the gist of the foregoing observations is a bit complicated.

But it is the case that people, in their definitions of consciousness, cannot include what they are not aware of. Some have indicated that this difficulty descends out of how consciousness works in the complicated ways it does.

But more obviously, this is how VERSIONS of consciousness are worked up here and there, hence codified into frames of reference, and which then ultimately serve, as they may, on behalf of this or that reality box.

Admittedly, this kind of version-making activity, ongoing everywhere, is one of the functions WITHIN consciousness per se, but which activity clearly cannot be taken as the single whole of it. But IF this kind of activity were to consist of the whole of consciousness, then consciousness would consist only of the parameters made of it here and there.

The implication is that there is no universal, innate consciousness in our species, and that consciousness is only a by-product of what people have become aware of, and then only with respect to the surrounding local situations within which they find themselves.

This kind of thing would end up, as it has, as a towering pile of many confusions not only with respect to what consciousness IS, but also what it SHOULD be or consist of, or how it is to be measured.

This is made further complicated because on average, and throughout history down until today, it seems that people do not wish to incorporate into their versions (reality boxes) of consciousness whatever they have not become impressively aware of themselves via self-experiencing.

216

There does not appear to be too much difficulty with respect to the meanings of "parameter," largely because it refers to how things are measured, estimated, or understood.

Indeed, since Day One of civilized human existence, it seems that our entire species has been totally preoccupied with measuring everything possible, and even of finding subtle and invisible things to take "the measure of."

Measuring activity seems both a necessary and a good thing, because once the measured parameters are established, then words, terms, and concepts can be established for whatever has been measured.

This usually results in compartmentalizing this or that kind of knowledge, for if the measure of things is achieved, or even approximated, then it is assumed that knowledge about them has been acquired.

So, the whole of this seems straightforward and logical.

217

There is, however, a significant glitch in all of this, for something depends on whom, why, and where the parameters of things are measured, and – not the least of it – what kinds of reality boxes are involved.

Discussions relative to this glitch are usually avoided not only because of some obvious sociological reasons, but because knowledge, once established as such, is supposed to rank above, or be senior to, humans themselves.

Because of the latter reason, it is difficult to challenge whatever has been accepted and codified as KNOWLEDGE. This is especially difficult, and even volcanic, in the case of new knowledge packages that might put cracks into older ones.

This issue has been introduced here because existing knowledge packages to date about consciousness are quite limited – and therefore limiting to any observing intelligence that attempts to utilize them with respect to what consciousness IS.

218

However, when this glitch IS considered, then it becomes immediately apparent that things are neither measured nor established the same way here and there, and that many things never undergo measurement at all simply because there is no objective or necessary reason to do so.

This is especially the case with respect to what people are not aware of in the first place, and which therefore cannot undergo measurement of any kind. Thus, taking the measure of something can only be achieved in the light of what people are aware of.

It is surely quite commonly understood that some people are aware of things that others elsewhere are not, and vice versa.

219

As some examples of this, the Tuareg people of Africa, whose environment is the great Sahara Desert, have traditionally taken the measure of some twelve kinds of winds, and the many kinds of sand. They have thereby assigned names and working frames of reference for them, for which there are no equivalents in English.

Likewise, the older Eskimo cultures have taken the measure of at least seventeen kinds of snow and their implications. In cultures traditionally dependent on camels as modes of transportation, an extensive list of different kinds of those beasts, plus the vagaries of camel attitudes, has long been available.

Again, in the older oceanic cultures of the Polynesian islanders, many different kinds of ocean waves were identified, along with, most importantly, their probable portents.

In cultures that need not be intimately familiar with subtle differences of wind, sand, snow, camels, and ocean waves, all winds are generally and simply seen as wind, sand as sand, and so forth.

During the gold rush decades in the wild American west, many mountaineers, explorers, and miners found they could sense danger and in what direction it lay or was coming from. This is to say nothing of the original Amerindians who, it seems, could sense just about anything in any direction, even at a distance of dozens of miles away.

Further back in time in ancient India, yoga texts identify dozens of different aspects or types of mind and of consciousness via Sanskrit terms for which there are no equivalents in English or other European languages. So, it impossible to really discuss those types except by reducing them to the few English terms that often do not even approximate the Sanskrit ones.

The same is the case with the older Urdu, Mongolian, and Tibetan languages all of which contain frames of reference for types of mental activity and kinds of consciousness that have never been identified by exact English equivalents. The original linguistic terms can of course be used. But any explaining of them has to be done via available English words and frames of reference, and in most cases the English explanations cannot approximate the original meanings.

This author can identify at least ten different types of empathy and an equal number of kinds of telepathy, and postulate the existence of about eighteen more.

But discussing these nuances is really difficult because any combination of English words still does not serve very well. In English, all kinds of empathy are, without further refinement, just empathy, and all types of telepathy are just telepathy, or perhaps, mind-to-mind, or ambiguous powers of mind. Indeed, the concept of powers-of-mind is almost always said in the plural. But no refined list that distinguishes among such powers has ever come into existence.

So, along with wind just being wind, camels just being camels, telepathy is just telepathy. Merely labeling manifold kinds of telepathy as just telepathy does not enable needed distinctions of the many kinds of it.

And neither does labeling consciousness as just consciousness, for indeed consciousness is altogether composed of many different aspects, or parts, or functions within it, to say nothing of the astronomical number of ever-changing reality boxes formatted within it.

220

HISTORICAL TIDBIT. With respect to the discussions in this book, the term CONSCIOUSNESS came into English usage at only about 1632 when it was first put forth as "consciousness of mine own wants."

Although this first English nuance was to undergo later modifications, it still remains a very recognizable measure of consciousness the parameters of which extend only so far as the self and the "wants" a self might have consciousness of. Sounds somewhat depressingly familiar, doesn't it?

The first nuance was somewhat later amended, but still within the contexts of self, to read: "Internal knowledge or conviction; knowledge for which one has testimony of within oneself, especially of one's innocence, guilt, deficiencies, etc." This, too, is rather familiar, isn't it?

It was not until about 1746 that CONSCIOUSNESS was radically redefined away from a strictly selfic basis as "The state or fact of being mentally conscious or aware of anything."

By far and large, this remains the dominant psychological and popular definition of consciousness. But this means that as of 2003 the essential conceptualization of consciousness has not changed during the intervening 254 years.

This definition is, to say the least of it, an intensely romantic and magical notion, and it is therefore understandable why it has held tremendous sway for so long.

221

But even so, some subtle situations rather buried within this romantic notion have been recognized by others trying to research the nature of consciousness.

Perhaps the first of these is that if human consciousness is "being mentally conscious or aware of anything" (i.e., also potentially of everything), then consciousness per se is NOT amenable to having its measure taken, the implication being that it is not only endless but also infinite.

This author indeed hastens to state that he has no problem with this in principle. However, there are outstanding factors to be considered, especially if one "wants" to develop one's consciousness, or to get out of one's limiting box.

222

Certainly, one of the factors involved, which has earlier been discussed from several points of view, is the now known fact that what might be called the sum total of human consciousness consists of more than enters the state of "being mentally conscious of."

During the twentieth century it has certainly become clear that the larger part of human consciousness is, as it were, non-conscious or sub-conscious – i.e., outside or beyond the state of being mentally conscious of.

Additionally, although one might indeed have the potential of "being mentally conscious or aware of anything," it is more to the point to observe that individuals far and wide (and throughout history as well) are, on average, NOT mentally conscious or aware of too much of anything, much less of everything.

Thus, there are some discrepancies between the romantic idea of boundless consciousness per se and how various aspects of it do or do not emerge in individuals.

223

Such discrepancies have been noticed by many others, especially during the first three decades of the twentieth century. And this may be one reason why definitions of consciousness were DOWNGRADED with respect to how to take some kind of measure of it.

First of all, consciousness was more completely linked to the definition of CONSCIOUS, to wit: "Having mental faculties undulled by sleep, faint, or stupor-awake."

Thus follows the definition of CONSCIOUSNESS, which is more or less compatible with that of conscious: "Mental awareness of the state or fact of being conscious of an external object, state, or fact; and especially of something within oneself."

224

Within the contexts of these definitions, it has long been taken for granted that the question of what consciousness IS has been correctly and completely portrayed.

But, believe it or not, there is yet another subtle problem with these definitions. The term CONSCIOUS was inducted into English from the Latin CONSCIUS which meant "with knowing."

From this emerges the subtle, and largely unacknowledged, problem having to do with knowing WHAT, and this problem can easily be superimposed on conscious OF what, and consciousness OF what.

225

If the point being made above is grasped, then it is possible to see that consciousness, and experience of it, is being defined by collapsing the definitions into the LIMITS of what one knows or is conscious of or, for that matter, what one has frames of reference for.

So, the question thus emerges as to whether human consciousness, and its sum total, should solely be defined via such limits in the face of many elements of consciousness known to transcend them.

Such seems a little silly, largely because the sum of human experiencing clearly establishes that there is a lot that is not known anywhere, a lot that has not yet been discovered, a lot that anyone has never been conscious of, and a lot that some have consciousness of, but which others do not.

In the light of the definitions presented above, it is possible to think that existing and accepted knowledge about consciousness has, well, some knowledge vacuums in it, together with an almost total lack of refinement of its manifold characteristics.

We do not yet know what human consciousness altogether and actually is, except to say that certain aspects can be superficially measured within the contexts of knowledge limits as established via the definitions discussed above.

But this is almost the same as saying that everyone experiences consciousness only within the contexts of their own experiential limits.

Thus, what they do not experience within such limits is simply not experienced as consciousness of anything, and certainly not of everything endless and infinite.

Chapter Thirty-Four

UPGRADING THE IMPORTANCE OF INNATE HUMAN SENSITIVITIES AVERAGE, ULTRA, AND SUPER

226

FOR REASONS that are not at all clear, the issue of human sensitivities is hardly ever incorporated into definitions of consciousness, or, for that matter, into definitions of mind. Even when human sensitivities are considered in their own contexts, treatment of them is usually minimal and narrow.

The exclusion is quite remarkable, in that if one does not sense something, then awareness of it does not take place, and thereafter mind and consciousness cannot become involved.

Of course, it is often assumed far and wide that much can happen to us that we at first do not sense and therefore do not expect, and so such lack of sensing is often thought of not only as a usual thing, but as natural.

227

This lack of sensing might also be attributed to sensing faculties and systems that are operating in latitudes far beneath the sum of their higher potentials.

Indeed, if one studies human sensing systems from the species level, it will be seen that different cultures and reality boxes nourish different ranges of sensitivities that others do not.

But when the ranges are combined, tabulated, and taken altogether, their sum indicates the real existence of a species innate spectrum of sensitivities that is not only impressive, but also quite extraordinary and awesome.

It is THIS far-ranging spectrum of sensitivities that can be thought of as natural and in-dwelling in everyone — IF it is remembered that all individuals are first born of the species BEFORE they are inculcated into this or that different cultural or social reality-box, after which the full spectrum of sensitivities disappears in favor of local and limited versions about what sensitivity consists of.

228

So, one principal, and quite hidden, reason for the minimal treatment of sensitivities appears to turn on the sociological issue of what people should be, or not be, sensitive to. After all, many societal reality boxes can be identified whose contexts require the nurturing and development of certain INSENSITIVITIES.

For example, war enthusiasts and arms merchants need to develop, within their reality boxes, certain amounts of insensitivity with respect to body counts and other formats of destruction and waste.

It would seem that the development of reality-box insensitivities is more paramount than the nurturing of sensitivities. If this be the case, it then follows that the treatment of human sensitivities needs to be confined and retracted to within minimal and narrow treatment.

229

In order to proceed with the discussions in this section, it is necessary to spotlight at least one sensitivity that is shared by vast numbers of the people, but which, throughout history, has received official negative treatment.

This is the sensitivity via which people in all walks of life come to feel, or intuit, that they are More than they have turned out to be, but the sum of which feeling seldom becomes a social issue of any real importance.

<h2 style="text-align:center">230</h2>

There are some historical examples where the More-thing did take on social importance, although only temporarily so. One such example, which stands for many others, involves the now ancient Roman Empire whose greatness still continues to be historically admired, often with great affection.

Whatever its greatness, that Empire was founded and maintained upon extensive dimensions of slavery, the enormous populations of which were derived not only from within but also from the numerous nations the Empire had conquered and enslaved. Many slaves felt that they were at least More than just slaves. So, many of what are euphemistically remembered as slave "rebellions" constantly got underway, at least two of which were large enough to almost bankrupt the Empire before things could be returned to the "greatness" perspective of the Roman norm.

<h2 style="text-align:center">231</h2>

Regarding the larger picture of the More-thing, the situation constantly arises within which people, especially subservient ones, should not be encouraged to find out, or to realize, that they are More.

With respect to this, there emerges an important saying, to wit: "What the people don't know, don't tell them." I.e., the people are not sensitive to what they don't know, but if you tell them what they don't know they will become sensitive to it.

So, in general people are told about only what they "need to know." Something along these lines HAS been discovered by conspiracy theorists, many of whom do correctly identify matters being withheld or covered up by those instigating conspiracies to do so.

Generically speaking, "The people" consist of all those beneath their higher-ups, the latter of which determine what the lower-downs should know or not know, or become sensitive to.

During thousands of years, it has turned out that this policy has proven to be the very best and easiest way to keep people in their lesser-informed, thus lesser sensitive, reality boxes.

The historical social reasoning and logic behind the policy proceeds from questioning how the people can be kept in their places that best benefit their higher-ups.

In this respect, the concept of "the people" is converted into, say, slaves, workers, wage earners, lesser functional officials, etc., and, as well, breeders of millions of disposable and replaceable "soldiers" who fight and die in whatever wars are designated by their higher-ups.

From this scenario, the on-going existence of which can easily be confirmed (even in times of peace), it appears that there are two major kinds of reality boxes: those that are more informed, and those that are lesser informed, down to the degree that some lesser reality boxes are barely informed at all, and thus not sensitive to too much.

232

If the dynamics of this scenario are identified and studied in depth, it turns out that there is a subtle and continuing problem within it.

The problem has to do NOT with what the people can socially be conditioned into with respect to agreeably occupying their lower status orders and assigned places in various power systems. Rather, the problem develops with respect to what the people might somehow come to think of themselves AS at some more PROFOUND level outside of whatever social conditioning that has been applied to them, and to which they have adapted.

This problem has, in part, always been resolved by not introducing too much profundity about anything into lesser-informed reality boxes – which occasionally tends to trickle upward into the reality boxes of the higher-ups, and/or into the reality boxes of those aspiring toward higher-up status.

233

In any event, avoiding or banishing profundity has usually been agreeably achieved, because profundity, when introduced into non-profundity reality boxes does not comfortably resonate within them. This, of course, results in cultures that deal only with the superficial. But never mind, because the goal of desensitizing sensitivities has been achieved – even though profound reality structures are seldom achieved.

234

However, if reality boxes of all waters are carefully examined, it turns out that there is one profundity that will begin resonating within them across the boards.

This is the profundity having to do with the real reality that one is MORE than one thinks, has been nurtured to be, or has been taught – MORE in terms of sensitivity, awareness, intelligence, mind, and consciousness.

It resonates because one's innate systems already know this deep within THEIR profound levels, even in the face of any or all subsequent reality boxes that have been manufactured in the limited light of this or that socio-environmental situation or condition.

235

The foregoing discussion serves as a brief background against which the feeling of being More than one is, or has been taught that one is, can be somewhat enlarged upon.

Although there are no statistics as to how many might have this particular sensitivity. It is often commented upon in various publications, and if you ask around, it seems to sit at some inscrutable tip of other than ordinary or average consciousness.

236

There is now an essential question to be asked. How is it that individuals can begin to feel that they are More than they have turned out to be, that they have potentials that extend beyond, and cannot fit into, the limited reality boxes they have adapted to in the normal, usual course of their socio-cultural development?

It is admittedly difficult to bring answers to this question. But there is one element in all of this that is certainly quite clear, i.e., that such individuals have somehow become self-SENSITIVE to the More-thing issue – and THIS in the face of all social desensitizing and insensitizing that otherwise affect their reality boxes.

Sensitivity to the More-thing is so universal that it is almost ubiquitously present behind all social scenarios, implying that there is more to human sensitivities than has been thought. And so the issue of sensitivities really does need to be up-graded out of its hereto minimal visibility.

237

SENSITIVE, as so far understood, is defined as: "Receptive to sense impressions; subject to excitation by external [and internal] agents."

SENSITIVITY is defined as: "The quality or state of being sensitive; the capacity of an organism to respond to stimulation."

It can be seen right away that if one has no sensitivity with respect to something, then one cannot easily or at all respond to it, much less take it into consideration and thoughtfulness.

HYPERSENSITIVE is defined as: "Excessively or abnormally sensitive or susceptible."

There is also a useful definition for the term SENSIBLE, albeit given as "archaic" (i.e., passé and no longer used), to wit: "Tending to produce an acute emotional response either negative or positive." Exactly why this definition should be considered archaic is something of a mystery, isn't it?

SUPERSENSIBLE is defined as: "Being above or beyond that which is apparent to the senses."

238

The creepy-crawly presence lurking within all of these definitions is, of course, the term "abnormally" – ABNORMAL being defined as: "Deviating from the normal or average."

It must be noted that the foregoing definitions were laid down during the early modernist scientific period when "the senses" were defined as only consisting of and confined to the five physical ones. They did not refer to, or even suggest, that "mental senses" existed.

Even so, concepts of the mental senses had always existed here and there, especially in Eastern and Western "mysticism." But in early scientific modernism, the mental senses were subsumed under the general heading of intelligence, and thereafter were never heard of again as such.

One reason for this probably turned on the fact that mental senses per se were not amenable to measurement — because there were so many of them, and discrimination among so many was difficult to determine. Another reason was that intelligence could, it was thought, not only be measured but standardized via intelligence testing, better known as IQ tests.

239

For additional clarity regarding the concept of "abnormal," NORM is defined as: "An authoritative [or authoritarian] standard or model; a principle of action binding upon members of a group and serving to guide, control, or regulate proper and acceptable behavior."

Thus, the definition of NORMAL is achieved, which is: "According to, constituting, or not deviating from a norm, rule, or principal," or, for that matter, not deviating from authority whatever THAT is composed of.

Without too much question, "an authoritative standard or model binding upon members of a group" clearly equates to a shared reality box, within which only "normal" sensitivities that "guide, control, or regulate proper and acceptable behavior" within the box are needed, desired, or, or course, required.

Any hyper-and super-sensitivities would only be bothersome, unwelcome, and not NEEDED, since they would tend to confuse the otherwise basic, less-profound, and normalizing frames of reference upon which the contours of a so-called normal reality box depend.

240

The ultimate implications of this clearly establishes (1) that a good deal of desensitizing of human sensitivities has been going on for a very long time; and (2) that the full spectrum of human sensitivities has never seen the light of day.

Although "normal" or "average" sensitivities might be studied, such studies are automatically limited by the "normal" contexts that prescribe what the sensitivities should or should not be.

Furthermore, and perhaps more technically speaking, "norms" are ostensibly and statistically based on what it is thought that most people experience, and thereby the sociological "average" can be conceptually identified as "an approximating arithmetic mean in being about half-way between extremes."

However, whatever is only "about halfway between" is always a lower-order BENEATH what is possible. Because of this, and with respect to consciousness overall, it is to be wondered if innate human sensitivities should be measured in such a way that reduces them to some lower order about half-way beneath what they otherwise innately consist of.

This kind of measuring DOWN to an average mean, clearly obliterates recognition of ultra- and super-sensitivities, the realization of which might actually be of extreme importance and relevance.

As it is, it can be wondered what our species would be like in the absence of sensitivities. Part of this wonderment can be filled in by examining reality boxes in which there apparently are more insensitivities than sensitivities, or in which a great deal appears to have undergone desensitizing.

241

At any rate, it is also to be wondered if one can get of the box by remaining only within the contexts of their "average" insensitivities. Clearly, a re-tooling of one's box means reopening up to More-thing sensitivities, this a project that was once referred to, during the 1950s, as "opening up the manifold doors of perception."

One interesting method of sensitivity re-tooling is simply trying, in private, to make more or less honest lists of what one IS sensitive to – and then to study such lists with respect to noticing what sensitivities are not included therein. Some new insights might thereafter occur.

Chapter Thirty-Five

UPGRADING DEFINITIONS OF MIND?

242

AS WE HAVE SEEN, human sensitivities were not included in the general definitions set up for consciousness and mind. One possible reason for the exclusion is that there are very numerous and multiple kinds of sensitivities, many of which remain vague, making it difficult to precisely identify them, even when they are experienced.

For example, the sources of those strange-mind filaments referred to as insights, inspirations, and hunches usually remain vague, and so no one knows exactly where they come from, although they obviously arise from sensitivities of some kind.

Because the exact nature of sensitivities remains elusive, it is difficult to establish general definitions for them that could fit with the general definitions of consciousness and mind.

So, they were excluded, for if they were to be included then the general definitions of consciousness and mind would have to undergo some extensive alterations.

The early failure to integrate sensitivities into the general definitions of consciousness and mind clearly suggest that those definitions, although not necessarily wrong in so far as they go, are nonetheless incomplete.

243

In any event, one can read existing definitions of consciousness and mind and not at all notice that there is yet another element that is not included in them.

It is "information," the essence of which is clearly compatible with any and all elements of innate consciousness and mind – with the exception of various kinds of reality boxes that have become structured so as to not only exclude this or that kind of information, but various kinds of sensitivity as well.

This failure can be forgiven somewhat, largely because the Age of Information Theory, as we now realize it, did not really get going until the 1930s when the American scientist, Claude E. Shannon (1916-2001), formulated a mathematical theory to explain aspects and problems of information and communication.

244

Before the 1930s, the concept of information had been around for quite some time, at least back into antiquity, and perhaps even into pre-history.

If one takes consciousness and mind into account, then it is quite obvious that at least one of their larger principal communal functions is to deal with information. Since the concept of information has been around, possibly since Day One, it is somewhat difficult to comprehend why it was not somehow incorporated into the general – hence standard – definitions of consciousness and mind.

245

HISTORICAL TIDBIT: In English, the term INFORM is taken from the Latin IN + FORMA, which meant "to put into [a] form."

The term INFORMATION appeared in English at about 1387 at which time it referred to "formation or moulding of the mind or character, training, instruction, or teaching; communication of instructive knowledge."

Somewhere between 1490 to as late as 1890, the foregoing definition seems to have dropped out of sight in favor of "Knowledge communicated concerning some particular fact, subject, or event; that of which one is apprised or told; intelligence, news."

At some point either before or after the 1890s, there

emerged the definitions largely depended upon through the twentieth century, to wit: "Knowledge obtained from investigation, study, or instruction; communication or reception of knowledge or intelligence; intelligence, facts, data, news."

246

Within the contexts of THIS book, it can be wondered why the 1387 definition referring to "formation or moulding of the mind or character via training, instruction, or teaching" disappeared from view, and, as well, disappeared as a frame of reference.

One possible reason is that the "formation or moulding" part of that definition is also the bottom line with respect to formatting, putting into a form, and constructing reality boxes in the minds of others via training, instruction, etc. If so, then this definition stands as one of the earliest blueprints, in English, for fundamental reality-box making.

247

To be sure, peoples everywhere undergo some kind of training, instruction, or teaching, and in fact, if they are aware enough, they will want to do so.

Additionally, not only is the innate mind quite pre-prepared to automatically accept any kind of training, instruction, etc., but those undergoing such fully expect to acquire knowledge that way.

To be equally sure, along with the training, instruction, and teaching, the outlines of reality boxes are acquired and solidified, especially with respect to local influential and powerful social contexts.

As has been discussed earlier, but to reemphasize here, something of all this depends not only on what such training and teaching consists of, but also on what it does NOT consist of.

And these two entirely connected factors lead, in turn, not only to social control, or at least supervision, of knowledge, but also to what "the people," in their various status levels, should or should not acquire knowledge of.

248

For clarity, although "the people" need be allowed to undergo training, instruction, and teaching for the benefit of various social groupings and relevant contexts, the general understanding is that their minds should work WITH whatever knowledge is thereby acquired.

What they should not realize too much about, however, is that their minds are also being shaped and, if the shaping is successful, then ultimately concretized in the process.

Indeed, almost any in-depth study of social power structures everywhere, and throughout human history, reveals that mind shaping is always considered the prerogative of the higher-ups because they are in possession of alpha reality boxes all others must carefully observe and submit to.

Thus, if "the people" don't know that mind-shaping also comes along with whatever knowledge they acquire, then don't tell them.

249

This means that the earliest English definition of INFORMATION first put forth in 1387 as "formation or moulding of the mind and character" was entirely inconvenient to, yes, mind-shapers everywhere, whether overt or covert.

So you can almost bet your bottom dollar that this was the reason that particular definition was phased out of view, and was not thereafter included in subsequent definitions of mind, or in definitions of information, for that matter.

250

There things more or less stood regarding definitions of mind and consciousness until the advent, during the 1930s, of Information Theory, the whole of which is quite technical in character, and which takes some stiff upper lips to comprehend.

Briefly, the Columbia encyclopedia indicates: "In this theory, the term INFORMATION is used in a special sense; it is a measure of the freedom of choice within which a message is selected from the set of all possible messages. Information is thus distinct from meaning, since it is entirely possible for a string of nonsense words and a meaningful sentence to be equivalent with respect to information content.

"Numerically, information is measured in bits. One bit is equivalent to the choice between two likely choices. The greater the information in a message, the lower its randomness, or 'noisiness'. A message [i.e., a coherent signal] proceeds along some channel from some source to the receiver; information theory defines for any given channel a limiting capacity or rate at which it can carry information, expressed in bits per second.

"The theory further shows that noise, or random disturbance of the channel, creates uncertainty as to the correspondence between the received signal and the signal transmitted. It is shown that the net effect of noise is to reduce the information capacity of the channel."

However, if the coherency of the signal and the coherency of the channel are compatible, then it is "more likely that the message [bits] can be reconstructed at the receiver without error."

Using various mathematical means, Claude E. Shannon, who first enunciated the theory, "was able to define channel capacity for continuous signals such as music and speech."

While the theory "is not specific in all respects, it succeeds remarkably in outlining the engineering requirements of communication systems and the limitation of such systems."

251

Well, now! We quickly need an example of something that aids in understanding the foregoing, while at the same time remaining consistent with it.

Much has earlier been made in this book about reality boxes which are obviously formatted upon given or selected frames of reference usually acquired via training, instruction, or teaching.

If we can think a frame of reference is a "channel" along which, or through which, information bits are processed so as to reach a "receiving" mind or consciousness, then it is possible to understand that when the incoming information AND the frame of reference are compatible, then the message might reach the receiving mind without too much error.

On the other hand, if the frame of reference is not compatible with the incoming message, then "noise" is encountered in the channel, and it becomes dubious that the information will reach the receiving mind without error, or perhaps not link up with it at all.

This kind of thing goes on all the time, especially when one offers certain kinds of information to someone else – and is rewarded only with a blank stare, or perhaps a bit of impatience or irritation.

In situations like this, it is all too common to think that the other person is a tad stupid. But more to the fact, the other person simply does not have frames of reference to certain kinds of information and therefore cannot process them.

252

In its early years, information theory was applied only to engineering requirements of physical communications systems.

At some point, the idea arose with respect to applying the theory first to the mind, and then to the human nervous systems as a whole, and which altogether are composed of a very great number of channels via which "information" is sent hither and thither throughout not only the physical body, to the mind, and hence into consciousness.

As will be enlarged upon ahead, the results of this work are still ongoing and accumulating.

The results so far more than suggest that the "old" definitions of mind and consciousness are clearly due for some upgrading, and also for some strategic reconceptualizing – which should deeply interest anyone trying to get out of the box.

Chapter Thirty-Six

UPGRADING DEFINITIONS OF CONSCIOUSNESS?

253

AS HAS BEEN reviewed earlier, the modern West fell under the sway of philosophical materialism that was defined as "a theory that physical matter is the only reality and that all being and processes and phenomena can be explained as manifestations and results of matter."

This quickly led to the concept [and doctrine] that only the five physical senses were real, because their processes could be explained as manifestations and result of matter. In the contexts of this book, the latter is, of course, a subsidiary reality box within the larger one of materialism.

254

Now, behind these two reality boxes, there are two subtle aspects that are seldom brought into the light of day. MATTER is officially defined as "the substance of which a physical object is composed" and "a substance that constitutes the observable universe and together with energy forms the basis of objective phenomena." What is not included in the official definitions, however, is that matter, in the contexts of materialism, is thought to be permanent and enduring, and as such does not therefore transcend itself.

When this context is applied to the permanency of the five physical senses, anything that transcends their physical limits can therefore not be explained within the "only reality" of physical manifestations of matter.

255

The whole of this has always required some decision-making at least among doctrinaire advocates not only of philosophical but also of scientific materialism. It was thus early decided that anything suggestive of the smell of transcendentalism should NOT be studied, because it could not be "real" within the contexts of the "only reality of physical manifestations of matter."

So, in order to cleanse the boards of the "only reality," and to keep it unadulterated by the not-real, a large number of phenomena thought to transcend the physical were simply swept aside by decree, since no examination of them was needed or would be useful to the accumulation of "real" knowledge.

Two familiar examples of what was disposed of are: a very large number of human sensitivities and the whole of the strange mind, the latter including recognizable potentially valuable items such as insight, intuition, telepathy, and knowledge "received" without the aid of advance study.

What was also disposed of, but not generally understood, was not only any interest in what people actually experience, but also consciousness itself which only, so to speak, inhabits people, and which was NOT thought to be a concomitant of the physical universe.

256

As it has turned out, scientific materialism has produced many wonders, including the technological and electronic age we all now live in, whether one likes it or not. It has also produced many technological horrors as is well known.

But there have been some significant fatalities along the way. Philosophy has, in general, bit the dust, largely because it cannot proceed creatively and insightfully too far by first excluding certain human phenomena pre-judged as not "real."

As already reviewed, sociology has "decomposed" for much the same reason, and in any event a vital sociology would be closely linked to vital philosophy, the latter, in turn, being closely linked to discovering what IS vital in the first place.

As to philosophical materialism itself, well, it is now largely considered at its dead end - because a philosophy of matter is not a real philosophy, but simply a matter of matter and what can be done with it.

257

When a given reality-box philosophy undergoes its demise, few take note either of its inherent fallacies or its passing largely because those who have interest in such matters are looking toward the arising of a new and vital philosophical power. It, too, will be a reality box, but it must contain frames of reference that were not only absent in the deceased one, but which also can be seen to project a future that seems worthwhile working toward. This might help explain the comeback of the same philosophy that materialism disposed of by simple decree.

This is, of course, the philosophy of TRANSCENDENTALISM "that emphasizes a priori conditions of knowledge and experience or the unknowable character of ultimate reality or that emphasizes the transcendent as the fundamental reality; also, the philosophy that asserts the primacy of the spiritual and transcendental over the material and empirical."

Please note the inclusion of the word "experience" in the above, another item that was considered useless in the disappearing philosophical reality box which, if not yet completely dead, is at least teetering on the final edge of its own "decomposition."

Also, in case one stumbles on it, the term A PRIORI is defined as "relating to or derived by reasoning from self-evident propositions." In turn, the definition of SELF-EVIDENT is given as "the quality of being evident with or without proof or reasoning."

In other words, what exists, exists, and does so with or without proof or reasoning, although what exists by its own self evidence can be submitted to reasoning, hence to examination.

TRANSCENDENT is defined as: "Extending or lying beyond the limits of ordinary experience; transcending the universe of material existence."

258

In the light of the above, the question emerges as to whether human consciousness can include transcendental experiencing. Oh, yes indeed, and this answer is self-evident, since so much of such experiencing goes on all of the time, and in all cultures, and in all ages.

However, Immanuel Kant (1724-1804), the German metaphysician and one of the greatest figures in Western philosophy, held that such experiencing was "determined by the mind's makeup," i.e., determined (as it might now be said) by reality boxes set up in the mind with respect to whether such experiencing should be experienced. Obviously (and one cannot resist this one last dig) the reality boxes of confirmed materialists should not permit transcendental experiencing in their internal workings, and if such might unfortunately occur, then it must not be admitted to.

259

The foregoing discussions now automatically loop back into the question of what people can sense and become sensitive to. And this, in turn, leads back into the issue of the five physical senses only, which, in their strictly physical contexts, cannot be seen as accessing information that is transcendental to them. THIS, in turn, leads to the question involving whether or not human nervous systems have innate senses other than the physical five.

HISTORICAL TIDBIT. Back in the 1930s when information theory was getting underway, another significant advance was taking place, this time in Germany, where the first electron microscope was invented, and improved upon in Canada and the United States.

The electron microscope did not utilize light rays going through optical lenses. Instead of light rays, it employed a stream of electrons controlled by magnetic or electric fields. This permitted greater magnification and greater depth of focus than the optical microscope and revealed more details of structure – for example, at the cellular level of living tissue.

Subsequently, the field-ion microscope (often thought of as

an electron microscope) was developed in the United States. If this is getting a bit heavy, all that needs to be understood about the field-ion microscope is that, when applied to metals, for example, their structure could be seen down to their atoms.

During the 1950s and 1960s, versions of the field-ion microscope, combined with other kinds of microscopes, made it possible to examine living biological cells down to levels never before imagined.

Because of this new capability, it was discovered, rather slowly and nervously to be sure, that every cell in a biological organism acts as some kind of receptor (or receiver) for SENSING some kind of "information."

After being sensed, the information, via innate electrical coding, is passed along from cell to cell, then through nervous system channels where it ends up in this or that control center which then makes "sense" of the electrical coding, and which is not always the brain.

It thus turns out that the entire human body is one gigantic series of sensing systems, having, as it does, millions upon millions of sensing receptors.

From all of this, it might impetuously be deduced that the five-senses-only concept is out the window. It is now understood that each of the five themselves have, in addition to their more usual work, specializing cells dedicated to sensing certain kinds of "information" that otherwise might be attributed to the strange mind only.

As was to be expected, interest soon arose with respect to identifying which cellular receptors received what kind of "information." So, numerous projects relative to this soon got underway in different research fields such as electro-chemical physiology; bio-radiation studies; hormone transmission; bio-electric information transfer; bio-electric field detection; pheromone and pheromone transfer; bio-subliminal perception; and neuromagnetic response.

260

For a number of years, this kind of work was reported only in scientific papers, whose ever-changing jargon is generally inaccessible to those not up to snuff with it, and which includes more than just a few of us.

However, in 1984, Robert Rivlin, a writer, and Karen Gravelle, a biopsychologist, teamed up to present the overall gist of receptor research, and produced an easy-to-read book entitled DECIPHERING THE SENSES: THE EXPANDING WORLD OF HUMAN PERCEPTION.

From this book, it can be learned that we have at least seventeen and more confirmed senses. To name just a few, we ALL have:

- Receptors in the nose that "smell" emotions, and that can identify motives, sexual receptivity, antagonism, and benevolence;

- Receptors in the ear that "hear" differences in pressure and electromagnetic frequencies;

- Directional finding and locating receptors in the endocrine and neuropeptide systems.

- Receptors for remote-sensing;

- Skin receptors that "recognize" the temperament of our own and other biological organisms;

- Receptors in the palms and soles of the feet that detect and recognize magnetic fields;

- Receptors that sense electrical energy;

- Whole body receptors that sense gravitational changes;

- Bio-electronic receptors for sensing radiation, including X-rays, cosmic rays, infrared radiation, and ultraviolet light.

- Receptors in the palms for sensing local and distant sources of heat;

- Receptors for telepathically sensing "languages" of nonverbal communicating;

- Receptors that trigger alarm and apprehension before their sources are directly perceived;

- Combined neural network receptors for telepathically sensing meaning of 130 nonverbal physical gestures and twenty basic kinds of nonverbal messages;

- Receptors that telepathically register nonverbal emotional "waves";
- In the pineal gland alone are receptors that keep track of light and darkness;
- Receptors anticipating with accuracy changes in the daily motions of sun and moon;
- Receptors that register solar flares and other disruptions;
- Receptors that sense coming earthquakes and storms (we share these receptors with farmers, cows, dogs, cats, and snakes).

If the pineal is fully functional, it can act overall as a nonvisual photo-receiver, this being perhaps the equivalent of the fabulous "X-ray" vision often noted in parapsychological experiments, and, under other terms, also made much of in Eastern mysticism.

Please note that this list is not complete.

261

All of these biological receptors, and more of them, are as innate as is consciousness innate, and each type of them exists somewhere along the inherent motherboard of consciousness, for if not, then no one would have them in the first place. Indeed, one can be quite sure that there are receptors that sense different kinds of wind, snow, waves, and even camel attitudes, since these can be seen to be active in various parts of the human world.

The only real problem with respect to all these innate receptors seems to focus on the nurturing and development of the conscious sensitivities that go along with them. If such sensitivities are not nourished and enhanced, then although the receptors do their work anyway, no one experiences them – except perhaps in dreams, some kind of trance-like state, or perhaps in some spontaneous or fortuitous type of strange mind experiencing.

262

As can now be seen, the standard, and "old," definitions of consciousness are not compatible with what has been discussed in this section, the substance of which is drawn from multitudes of scientific papers which anyone can track down if they are up to the challenge.

Thus, much like the "old" definitions of mind, those for consciousness ought to undergo some extensive reality box re-thinking.

PART EIGHT

HUMAN CONSCIOUSNESS INTO THE FUTURE

Chapter Thirty-Seven

INFORMATION THEORY MEETS BIO-RECEPTORS OF THE HUMAN NERVOUS SYSTEM

263

WHAT WAS ONCE called "thought transference," but which thereafter was dubbed "telepathy," was attributed to the strange mind. The reason for this was that it transcended the "laws" of physical matter in so far as those laws were understood.

Since this understanding was generated within what became an alpha reality box insisting that matter was the "only" reality, telepathic experiencing, as well as the strange mind as a whole, could be ejected from any present and future consideration. The strategy did not prevent telepathic experiencing from happening, of course, especially the vivid and well-documented kind via which mothers could sense when their children were in danger.

The ejecting also did not put an end to another meaningful kind of strange mind phenomena. This involves well-documented cases where an individual suddenly jumps out of the way of some mortal threat, and does so BEFORE having any conscious realization either of the threat or the jumping.

The existence of such transcending phenomena is self-evident, especially if one experiences them. But even so, if matter was the "only" reality, the phenomena could, by decree, be ejected from consideration.

264

Because of all this ejecting, an important question surfaces, to wit: Can those researching information theory to human nervous systems, and those researching full-field bio-receptors, ethically eliminate, in advance, certain phenomena from consideration?

Obviously, they cannot – if they are to proceed in achieving and confirming discoveries implicit in their work.

265

As briefly listed earlier, innate receptors in the physical body and its nervous systems have been identified with respect to certain kinds of telepathy and remote-sensing, as well as receptors that trigger alarm and apprehension before their sources are directly perceived – if, of course, one is somehow sensitive to the information bits such receptors are identifying and conveying.

Although receptors do exist, they convey their "messages" into the whole of the nervous system as information bits, after which, it might logically be expected, the information emerges into conscious awareness and perception of it in a straightforward way – which is to say, emerges into the neo-cortex in the brain, which is the "seat" of conscious perception, especially during the waking state.

266

However, information theorists have been on the case for quite some time, and it turns out that what might be straightforward is almost anything but. Here, then, is a completely different saga, indeed.

The intricate details of this saga have been collected and collated into an astonishing 1991 book entitled THE USER ILLUSION: CUTTING CONSCIOUSNESS DOWN TO SIZE, by Tor Norretranders, Denmark's leading science writer. The book is something of a challenge to read, but a few of its main highlights can usefully be pointed up.

First of all, it is to be understood that although we have receptor sensing systems that detect information, the information must be transferred along various channels so as to be received by a central control unit (which is commonly thought to be the brain), after which the information enters into the neo-cortex where cognitive perception takes place and where mental imaging and certain forms of understanding are generated.

What is not completely understood by many, is that in the transferring of the information, the information bits are first sent through a series of subconscious processing filters and lenses, the principal function of which is to decode (i.e., transliterate) the information BITS so that they can be related to or compared with whatever is stored in memory banks.

If this process is successful, the information is "recognized," and an "understanding" cognitive perception of it can take place in the neo-cortex. If memory storage packages cannot be found, then "noise" occurs, and the transliterated information cannot achieve cognitive perception, except, possibly, in some garbled form.

In psychology, the whole of the subconscious processing filters and lenses, and the memory components involved, is accepted as psychological components of the mind – although after a hundred years or so of modern psychological inquiry and research, very little has been discovered as to how and why the mind does all of this.

267

Information theorists do not bother themselves too much with psychological lenses, etc., or with the intricacies of the mind. Rather, they are interested in establishing how many information bits per second from any source enter into the overall nervous systems versus how many bits per second enter into the conscious-making part of the brain, i.e., the cortex (also called the neo-cortex).

As will be elaborated just ahead, much of the information that gets into the whole brain does NOT get forwarded into the cortex, which is the part of the brain that produces the conscious OF phenomenon.

It seems that information theorists first sorted this out in the 1950s. Our sensing systems receive an astronomical eleven million information bits per second.

But on the same per second basis, only an incredibly small (repeat, incredibly small) fraction of those bits manage to get through to the neo-cortex and trigger conscious awareness and perception therein.

What remains of the eleven million bits is "just thrown away." This overwhelming discrepancy has been reconfirmed several times. Indeed, in 1977 the famous brain researcher, Karl Popper (1902-1994), stated that "All experience is already interpreted by the nervous system a hundredfold – or a thousandfold – before it becomes conscious experience."

In other words, and to repeat, the subconscious or non-conscious parts of us are, in each second, receiving an astronomically significant amount of information, but in terms of conscious awareness and perception we "use" only a tiny fraction of it.

The title of Norretranders' book, THE USER ILLUSION, thus refers to the idea that if we think we use all information coming into our systems, this is indeed an illusion.

268

Obviously, information about what we are sensitive to, or have become sensitized to, has a better chance of entering into conscious realization, even if only partially so. Norretranders indicates that a good deal of information is pumping away just beneath complete awake conscious recognition of it.

So, he suggests that "we should trust our hunches and pursue our intuitions" because "they are closer to real information than the reality that is consciously perceived."

Yes! And in dreams, too, and in premonitions, and in many other kinds of strange mind phenomena. And many of those who have credited the reality of the strange mind have recognized this throughout the centuries.

Implicit in Norretranders' suggestion is the idea that all information bits that do not extend into the conscious awake state might not get completely "thrown away."

Such bits might lurk around, and might even trigger innate

aspects of consciousness that have not been nourished into sensitivity. Something like this might be going on beneath the consciously awake state, and occasionally erupt via a compelling spontaneous or fortuitous manifestation of various strange mind experiencing.

269

From all of this, a perfectly logical wonderment can arise. Why, for goodness' sake, do our innate sensing receptors intake such a vast amount of information bits, when the sum of what does get into neo-cortex awareness and cognition is miniscule? Some have opined that this is "natural," for otherwise we would be so flooded with information and go bonkers. Well, maybe.

But this is more than slightly uncharacteristic of all other innate human information systems that are otherwise quite intricate, precise, and highly organized in their functioning. To be sure, even psychological filters and lenses are highly organized, or they wouldn't work.

270

It is now appropriate to point up that psychological researchers and information theorists have so far not taken much interest in the topic of reality boxes and how and why they are formatted, as well as how they deal with information of any kind.

Reality boxes quite clearly belong to the category of filters and lenses, and are a full part of the pre-conscious processes that interpret, accept, or reject information before, as Popper indicated, "it becomes conscious experience" in the mind.

271

This is reminiscent of some of the observations of the great philosopher, Immanuel Kant, who was discussed earlier. Instead of assuming that our ideas, to be valid, must conform to an external reality independent of our knowing, Kant proposed that objective reality is known only insofar as it conforms to the essential structure of "the knowing mind."

What Kant proposed was entirely compatible with the earlier philosopher, also great, John Locke, who proposed much the same thing – that ideas, and how THEY are understood, stand between reality and any understanding of IT. For clarity, reality exists, of which the mind makes whatever reality-box ideas it can or does, and from which ideas are derived whatever understanding can be derived from the ideas.

272

Kant's concept of the "essential STRUCTURE of the knowing mind" surely refers to that part of the mind that knows things, and, equally surely, the knowing is composed, as Locke indicated, of ideas that the knowing mind assumes it knows.

Now, ideas absolutely have to be based in some kind of frames of reference, even if only vague or imagined. Ideas can then also generate additional frames of reference that are compatible with them.

From this, it can be thought that frames of reference equate to the "essential STRUCTURE of the knowing mind," and which structure thereafter equates to a reality box in whose contexts information is interpreted, accepted, or rejected "before it becomes conscious experience" in the awake conscious mind.

Thus, it might be that reality boxes, but not innate consciousness, would have trouble with too much information, and obviously so with respect to certain categories of it that are inconsistent with the realities of the reality box.

273

And here now emerges into at least a partial visibility the outlines of a great distinction between innate human consciousness and the knowing part of mind that houses reality boxes.

Information theorists and bio-receptor researchers have shown that our nervous systems are accessing millions of information bits every second. Information theorists have shown that only very small fractions of the millions enter into conscious awareness, and into the knowing part of the mind.

Since we can see that the millions of information bits are

radically reduced before they enter the knowing part of the mind, it seems quite clear that the accessing of the millions of bits belongs to innate functions and processes of consciousness itself.

It is helpful to make a good mental image of this. Just imagine a gigantic balloon that is inflated with millions of information bits. Then imagine a tiny hole somewhere on the surface of this gigantic balloon. There is a very tiny tube poking out of this hole, to which, at its other end, your conscious-making cortex is attached. A very tiny trickle of information bits is coming through this tube – and it is only the information contained in this trickle that one becomes conscious OF in the knowing part of the mind.

Most do not at all realize that they also have the gigantic balloon behind this small trickle.

Even so, the innate accessing of information bits into it is taking place each second regardless of what is going on in the knowing part of the mind, and certainly is taking place unbeknownst to the knowing part.

274

Even a brief survey of different kinds of reality boxes will reveal that they have trouble with various categories of information, especially with too much of it, and with particular information sets or packages that are at odds with their basic frames of reference.

Innate consciousness does not reject millions of information bits, but reality boxes do. Thus, the information problem is with reality boxes, not with innate consciousness itself.

275

So, yet another significant question arises, one having to do with WHY reality boxes are fabricated in the first place. This, too, must be a function of innate consciousness, or it would not happen.

One possible answer is that the innate consciousness of the human species is somehow innately structured so as to allow, or to facilitate, adaptation to ANY environments in which members of the species find themselves.

If this would be the case, then reality box frames of reference relevant to ANY different environments and situations within it would somehow have to be established in the knowing part of the mind.

For this innate consciousness activity to be entirely workable, innate consciousness faculties would also have to preexist with respect to enabling the changing, recombining, re-integrating, and upgrading of various kinds of knowing reality boxes when environments and situations alter – provided, of course, that reality boxes are flexible enough, rather than fixed like cement.

276

It is clearly suggestive of not only the bigness, but also of a bigger picture of innate human consciousness.

It does not seem to matter all that much when, at the human individual level, certain reality boxes go bonkers and victimize other reality boxes – because each time a new babe is born it is innately and inherently equipped with all of the "stuff" of innate consciousness. The "stuff" is thus forwarded at the species level via each generation born and their progeny, and then theirs, etc.

What follows thereafter is the history of reality boxes, all of which eventually come and go, recombine, if possible, but otherwise "decompose" and vanish. Such, of course, is NOT the history of innate human consciousness itself, but also, as is said in ancient Eastern mysticism, only temporary facets and reflections of it.

Thus, in the bigger picture of innate human consciousness, the kaleidoscope of the "wheel of rebirth" is always slowly turning, and forming new reality-box "patterns" as it does so.

Chapter Thirty-Eight

INNATE CONSCIOUSNESS RECOMBINANT

277

IN ITS September 29, 2001, issue (Vol. 160), SCIENCE NEWS, the esteemed journal that updates, in nutshell formats, on-going science activity on a weekly basis, published a surprisingly lengthy article by Bruce Bower, entitled "Joined at the Senses: Perception may feast on a sensory stew, not a five-sense buffet."

The overall gist of the article focuses on "a growing number of studies that tap into the brain's sensory cross talk. For many neuroscientists, these investigations light the way toward a solution to the fundamental mystery of how the brain unites separate sensations into multifaceted experiences. In their view, the brain somehow assembles separate sights, sounds, and other sensations into reasonable approximations of what's out there."

278

In the up-coming view of many neuroscientists, "interactions across sensory receiving areas in the cortex may be more widely spread than previously suspected." As a result, scientific "appreciation for brain cells that respond to two or more types of sensory input has expanded dramatically in the past several years. Researchers refer to such cells as multi-sensory, or multimodal, neurons" that "blend" together.

279

Furthermore, these intriguing [cellular] partnerships underscore the need to move beyond "simple models of cerebral organization."

Then comes the big blast (and here one must remember that this blast appears in SCIENCE NEWS): evidence on sensory mixing, however challenging to mainstream thinking about perception, indicates that "It's time to drop the assumption that people and other animals perceive the world through separate sensory channels of vision, hearing, touch, taste, and smell."

280

Multimodal, blending, mergering perception is not merely the primary type of perception. "It's the only type of perception." Whereas some cells in some brain areas respond strongly to a single type of sensory input, many more also react to inputs from multiple systems.

Furthermore, tests on infants reveal that their perceptual sensing systems deal with global and multi-sensory types of information beginning early in life.

The article concludes with the advisory that the question of whether unified sensory information (as a "sensory stew") actually exists and is used by perceptual systems "matters very much to both theory and research," to say the least of it.

281

In its October 19, 2002, issue (Vol. 162), SCIENCE NEWS published a follow-up, again by Bruce Bower, with respect to the "global" issue entitled "Spreading Consciousness: Awareness goes global in the brain."

GLOBAL is defined as "comprehensive, universal," but as used in the article's context, it refers to the entire brain, and whatever is entire to it.

The gist of this article focuses on brain activity observed via magnetic resonance imaging (MRI) scanning as volunteers performed memory, visual, or some other mental task.

One chief result, so far, of these brain-imaging studies

shows that bursts of neural-response activity in several far-flung areas of the brain occur before the tasks finally highlight discrete brain regions that exhibit dramatic surges of activity.

What this means, to some of the involved researchers anyway, is that consciousness eludes efforts of brain imagers to corral it into neural pens. This inspires some researchers boldly to argue that the seat of consciousness itself is not in the brain. Nevertheless, "There's a global brain state that's constantly in flux [as a sensory stew] and that creates conscious experiences," as contrasted to the issue of the totality of consciousness itself, wherever that totality might otherwise be found.

282

Now there is a concept, together with a precise word for it that has not been used in these two future-important articles.

That word is drawn from COMBINE defined as: "To intermix, blend: to possess in combination; or, to bring into close relationship."

RECOMBINATION is defined as: "The formation of new combinations."

Thus, RECOMBINANT refers to whatever "exhibits recombinations."

The two latter terms are presently being utilized with reference to genetic recombination, while the entire human genome is being seen as completely recombinant.

But both of these terms can equally be applied, without too much argument, to ever changing "sensory stews" out of which not only sensory perception, but different kinds of it, somehow takes place, if and when they do.

283

Referring back to section 13 (in which the many innate attributes of the human species entire are discussed), a large number of faculties or attributes are innate throughout our species, all of which involve different kinds of subsets of consciousness within the whole of it.

The innate attribute of language-making is perhaps the best known so far. That innate attribute is already prepared to recognize and deal with vocalized sounds and even syntax, out of which and because of which different languages emerge and can be learned.

But the whole of this clearly implies that the innate language attribute is already prepared to be, and is recombinant, simply because recombination of vocalized sounds and syntax is necessary in the case of different languages – of which some thousands currently exist, with many more having passed into obsolescence or into forgotten history.

284

By analogy, the innate attribute of language is something like a piano with its motherboard of eighty-eight keys. Different combinations and recombinations of the eighty-eight keys produce different sounds and melodies, and even different tempos and cadences, beats, sonorities, and modulations, together with not only their sonic waves, but also their mental ones, the whole of which can be endlessly recombined in a vast number of ways.

This is quite well understood, of course. But with respect to language research, it is easy enough to identify the different languages and to correctly attribute them to the innate language module in the motherboard of human consciousness.

The only real problem is that language researchers cannot yet find the language piano itself, which is apparently installed in the seat of consciousness, again not locatable so far.

285

In the current and on-going confusions about innate human consciousness and where its seat is to be discovered, there seems little reason NOT to apply this analogy, if only hypothetically, to the fuller and bigger scope of innate human consciousness itself.

However, the main motherboard of innate human consciousness probably has very many more than just eighty-eight keys because the many millions of recombinant human consciousness formats unambiguously attest as much.

286

In the hypothetical light of all this, innate human consciousness will somehow, in a very positive sense, always be recombinant into the future, perhaps even in defiance of temporary reality boxes that have black holes in THEIR consuming formats of consciousness.

So, there's always a future for our species, not so much because we have reality boxes, but because we have innate consciousness.

Science, like life, feeds on its own decay.
New facts burst old rules; then newly divined conceptions bind old
and new together into reconciling law.

William James
(1842-1910)

THE CODA OF HUMAN CONSCIOUSNESS INNATE

287

AS TO WHETHER human consciousness per se is innate in our species, well, debates and arguments can arise.

Even so, in the end, and in the bigger picture of all things, it is to be wondered what we (any of us) would be like without it.

288

If consciousness per se would not be innate in our species, thus existing in everyone born out of the species, then problems obviously arise having to do not only with how it otherwise comes into existence, but also regarding what it is.

If it is not innate, then various reality boxes, within the contexts of their frames of references, have a fair claim with respect to erecting concepts of what it consists of, or ought to.

289

However, in the bigger human picture, and as history attests, reality boxes "work" as they do only for as long as they do – after which, no matter how alpha they were during their times, they ultimately "decompose" and are replaced by successor boxes built out of quite different frames of references.

It cannot therefore be said that reality boxes forward consciousness itself into the future.

290

Rather, the forwarding of consciousness itself occurs via each subsequent generation born not only from their forbearers, but also out of the species itself.

Indeed, if, for its on-going survival, consciousness would be completely dependent only upon this or that reality box, then it too would "decompose" and vanish along with the reality boxes.

291

But this does not happen. The inescapable reason, and as everyone knows, is that when each new babe first opens its eyes it is already primed with primeval innate consciousness in advance of any subsequent reality-box imprinting that does or does not take place.

292

In musicology, a CODA refers to a concluding musical section that is formally distinct from the main structure of a musical composition, and which section can be repeated time and again.

Without too much trouble in doing so, this can also be applied to human life overall, the "main structure" of which is traditionally conceptualized as consisting of the sum of all human (reality box) activities that take place AFTER birth, and into which all of us enter in one fashion or another.

293

However, human "main structure" affairs continuously shift about, change, alter, swell up, peak, dwindle down, "decompose," and vanish – except where they may be recorded via "mythic" memory, or in some other form of notation that can be retroactively compiled into the official "history" of main-structure affairs, and which history is seen as all-important and meaningful.

294

But this is NOT the history of our species, or of the innumerable people born again and again out of it, most of whom are used up, wasted, consumed, made dead, and namelessly forgotten not on behalf of our innate consciousness, but on behalf of various reality boxes – which, as their times pass, are likewise used up, wasted, consumed, and made dead.

295

In the bigger picture of all human things, the "history" of main-structure affairs does present one advantage, albeit one seldom recognized, and if so, only in retrospect.

That "history" clearly establishes that negative black-hole types of reality boxes can be formed or fomented within human consciousness that ask for the destruction of whatever does not fit with them – and ask such via violence, terror, war, and sometimes genocide, and other "crimes against humanity," as it is fondly expressed.

But this again is merely only the history of conflicting reality boxes, not the history of innate human consciousness, which IS our species itself. Rather, the history of innate human consciousness is discernable by what is positively and pro-actively created and built out of it – even in the face of reality box deterrence and destructions.

296

When all of the main structure reality box activities are over and finished one way or another, then ALWAYS occurs the more relevant human coda, which, indeed, is a "musical" section that is formally distinct from the main structure of human activities – the coda of on-going innate human consciousness, which replays itself time and again no matter what has gone on in any of the main structures, and does so via each new generation born. Innate human consciousness continuously replicates itself anew this way.

Thus, IF human consciousness is not only innate, but also permanently geared, primed, and ready to create and build, all else that follows is merely a matter of reality boxes and the ultimate sums of their either positive or negative frames of references.

297

Additionally, IF innate human consciousness is permanently

primed and ready to positively create and build, but is not nurtured to do so within given social reality box contexts, the permanence STILL exists as potential within the total sum consciousness of everyone. Just because pro-active creative and building aspects are not nurtured is no sign that they have stopped existing as such.

This overall situation certainly plays some full part of the More-thing that individuals intuit or become sensitive to on their own behalf. In other words, the More is always innately there, even if it has not been nurtured or developed into pro-active expression and workability.

298

Although the discussions and observations in this book are now at an end, the existence of innate human consciousness is not.

Indeed, THAT consciousness flows through each reader, and, via each, then flows through not only "deep in," but also "far-out" dimensions of consciousness – whereby innate human consciousness recognizes itself as such, and whereby THAT self-recognized consciousness recognizes itself in everyone.

Without going outside,
you may know the whole world.
Without looking through the window,
you may see the ways of heaven.

TAO TE CHING
Lau Tsu, sixth century B.C.

SUGGESTED READING

NOTES OF EXPLANATION

It is often said that the more one learns about something, the more influence, control, and empowerment one has over it. There are numerous ways to learn about something, but two of those ways are usually considered most important.

The first involves organized intellectual "armchair" study of what is already known, and most formal educational curriculums focus on this approach. However, one must eventually go into the hands-on "open field" in which one finds what has been studied actually "at work." Thus, seeing and comprehending something actually at work is an important form of learning that increases direct experience and knowledge of it.

As discussed in the text, the topic of reality boxes is relatively new, and so human affairs are not yet specifically associated with reality boxes at work. So the workings of human affairs are portrayed as consisting of people doing what they do. But if the concept of reality boxes is introduced into the proceedings of human affairs, then it is possible to see and comprehend that the people involved are at work acting out the dynamics of their reality boxes.

There are many good books that are not only fascinating reads for the human-interest stories they tell, but which can also help increase recognition of reality boxes at work, usually in pursuit of power, sometimes ascending, sometimes tumbling down. A selection of such books is listed below, together with brief reviews of their contents showing why they should be studied in the light of reality box realities.

With respect to the strange mind, there is a large modern literature available. Most of it tends to focus not so much on the enormous strange-mind consciousness itself, but on the problems and difficulties of PSI researchers selectively attempting experiments within the contexts of their ideas, theories, and methods (i.e., in the contexts of THEIR reality boxes). Thus, the strange mind at work is seldom seen, except as it may or may not emerge in this or that research environment.

However, there are some few really great books that impartially document the strange-mind work, and which help increase overall recognition of its manifold and amazing phenomena. A short list of these is provided below, together with brief reviews of their contents.

TOWARD RECOGNIZING THE DYNAMICS OF REALITY BOX REALITIES

Anderson, Walter Truett, REALITY ISN'T WHAT IT USED TO BE. (Harper and Row, San Francisco, 1990). [Documents changing reality boxes about reality, how traditional societies created and maintained their ideas about the world, how postmodern artists, scholars, and scientists are exposing the workings of the reality-creating machinery, and how reality is packaged in various ways and to what ends it is.]

Bakker, Robert T., THE DINOSAUR HERESIES. (Kensington Publishing Co., New York, 1991). [Reviews dramatic reality-box wars among fossil dinosaur hunters. A good read, in that much the same goes on in all scientific disciplines. Was a best-seller.]

Bernstein, Peter L., THE POWER OF GOLD. (John Wiley & Sons, New York, 2000). [An excellent history of different kinds of reality-box obsessions involving gold. Many giggle factors, if one can see through the golden haze.]

Dixon, Norman F., SUBLIMINAL PERCEPTION: THE NATURE OF A CONTROVERSY, (McGraw-Hill, London, 1971). ["Controversy" usually implies reality-box conflicts and resulting scandals. As of 1971 and earlier, the reality boxes of many were opposed, including conventional scientists, to admitting to the existence of subliminal perception.

Dixon was the first to thoroughly examine the concept, and showed how it affects the human nervous system and influences aspects of behavior, but also affects perceived realities as well. Bit of a challenging read, but worth making the attempt.]

Dublin, Max, FUTUREHYPE, (Dutton, Penguin Books, 1991). [Via brilliant but scathing analysis, the author surveys what equates to reality-box thinking behind "those who make a career of blueprinting our future with 'expert' predictions," but which seldom come to pass. Reviews the psychology and ideology of futurology, both of which depend on reality-box orientations. Bit of a challenging read, not because of what is in the book, but because of the mind reading it. Highly recommended, though.)

Epstein, Edward Jay, THE RISE & FALL OF DIAMONDS.

(Simon and Schuster, New York, 1982). [A concise, blow-by-blow example of building a social reality box from the bottom up. The men, the giant cartel, and the campaign that convinced the world that "Diamonds Are Forever," and that every woman must have one to be socially acceptable. This WAS successful, since diamond sales thereafter went into the stratosphere. Great stuff.)

Epstein, Joseph, SNOBBERY: THE AMERICAN VERSION, (Houghton Mifflin, New York, 2002). [In one of its aspects, snobbery is defined as attempting to emulate what's "in," or as blatantly imitating, fawningly admiring, or in seeking, by contrived appearances, to be associated with those one regards as one's superiors, especially if they achieve success, fame, or social spotlights.

This emulating requires some kind of reality-box make-overs or modifications, even if they are only superficial ones. "Old" forms of snobbery are reviewed and "new" versions of it are described in highly entertaining and sometimes hilarious reality-box detail. Epstein wonders if snobbery might be a full part of human nature. A very good read.)

Friedman, Thomas L., THE LEXUS AND THE OLIVE TREE, (Farrar, Straus, Giroux, New York, 1999). [This book is subtitled "Understanding globalization," by which is implied that various non-global-thinking reality boxes will need to undergo readjustment if such understanding is to be acquired. The author's argument can be summarized quite simply. Globalization is not just a phenomenon and not just a passing trend. It is the international system that replaced the Cold War system.

Globalization is the integration of capital, technology, and information across national borders, in a way that is creating a single global market and, to some degree, a global village." Replete with vivid stories and a set of original terms and concepts necessary toward up-dating non-global-thinking reality boxes.]

Hooper, Judith and Dick Teresi, THE 3-POUND UNIVERSE. (Macmillan, New York, 1986). [Easy-to-read, time-line chronicle of reality-box wars with respect to "looking for consciousness" in the three pounds of Jell-O-like tissue of the human brain. Reviews many human details that science writing often ignores. Much of amusing interest to those interested in consciousness. Foreword by Isaac Asimov.]

Hughes, Robert, THE FATAL SHORE, (Alfred A. Knopf, New York, 1987). [Fascinating reality-box management and control behind the epic of Australia's founding. Writing is excellent, and the book describes sagas enough for ten movies.]

James, Lawrence, RAJ - THE MAKING AND UNMAKING OF BRITISH INDIA. (St. Martin's Press, New York, 1997). [Essentially, the 200-year-long saga via which traditional Indian social power and economic reality boxes were eroded and disposed of by clever British ones that became monolithic and magnificent. Lush with descriptive details. A basic textbook on how to wreck reality boxes that stand in the way of economic power grabs.]

Lord, John, THE MAHARAJAHS, (Random House, New York, 1971). [Intimate details of the staggering wealth and reality boxes of the Indian Maharajahs who once had their own armies, jewels valued in the highest millions, fabulous princes that gave India its golden age, their flagrant and exotic lifestyles, their sometimes divinity, their often excesses. The book is gossip rich, and a page-turner.]

Ludwig, Emil, THE NILE, (The Viking Press, New York, 1937). [Perhaps the best book ever written about the Nile River in Africa, covering its 4,000 miles and 6,000 years of history, its natural wonders aplenty, and the endless succession of human reality boxes along its course from ancient to modern times.]

Lynes, Russell, THE TASTE-MAKERS, (Harper & Brothers, New York, 1955). [If reality boxes can be engineered and made, so can the "makers" of artistic-like taste proceed. Lynes begins his coverage of American taste-making at about 1827, and then walks the reader through how taste (and snobbery) was established, changed, altered, and ultimately replaced by new tastemakers, with the many "victims" of taste-making struggling to keep up and emulate the new. A perfectly delightful read.]

Marks, Richard Lee, CORTES, (Alfred A. Knopf, New York, 1993). [Outstanding descriptions of epic reality-box clashes as the "great Spanish adventurer," Hernan Cortes, encounters the reality boxes of the Aztecs in ancient Mexico. Although a historical recounting, reads like a page-turning novel. Intimately lush in obscene details, and "the first in decades to draw on modern scholarship." What a gripping story!]

Seagrave, Sterling and Peggy Seagrave, THE YAMATO

DYNASTY, (Broadway Books, New York, 1999). [Although subtitled "The secret history of Japan's imperial family," this book is more about that nation's ruling power classes, whose reality boxes demonstrate tremendous powers of economic and social organization, and to which even the imperial family is largely subservient. As discussed in the book, these reality-box elements account for how and why Japan quickly recovered after World War II and became one of the world's richest nations. Yet another terrific read.]

TOWARD RECOGNIZING THE DYNAMIC REALITY OF STRANGE-MIND CONSCIOUSNESS

Bucke, Richard Maurice, COSMIC CONSCIOUSNESS, (First published in 1901, reprinted by University Books, New Hyde Park, N.Y., 1961). [Rightly considered to be one of the great classics of "mystical" experience, Bucke developed this book out of the onset, when he was 36, of his own strange-mind experiencing which he dubbed as "cosmic."

The experiencing comes suddenly without warning, during which, at its peak point, an intense intellectual illumination occurs presenting to the mind the meaning and drift of the universe. His own metaphysical experiencing led him to study similar experiences of other individuals and to formulate a theory of higher consciousness as an innate faculty in human consciousness. A major portion of the book is devoted to the massive and varied evidence of people, from the time of Moses onward, in whom strange-mind cosmic consciousness became active.]

Day, Harvey, SEEING INTO THE FUTURE, (Thorsons Publishers, London, 1966). [In keeping with the motto that facts should not be rejected because they seem incredible, the author indicates that "This book has been written not to convince anyone of the truth or accuracy of the predictive arts, but merely to set down predictions made that have come true. Wherever possible, facts have been checked," meaning that evidence of the predictions was in hand before what was predicted came to pass.

Reviewed are predictions made by some astrologers, palmists, and professional seers, but most impressively presented are dreams of ordinary individuals via which future elements appeared and ultimately came to pass. Much along these lines does not come to pass, of course, but much that does can be documented, and the instances presented in this book substantiate that somewhere and somehow there exists innate faculties in the strange-mind to foresee. One of the best reads of this genre.]

Dingwall, Eric J., ABNORMAL HYPNOTIC PHENOMENA, in four volumes, (J & A Churchill, London, 1967-1968). [Dingwall seeks to fill the gap in the literature of nineteenth-century cases of hypnotism and mesmerism. His aim was "raise the curtain on the almost unknown and forgotten activities of the mesmerists of the nineteenth century while concentrating on the paranormal (strange-mind) aspects of their work. The result is a treasure trove of seeing the strange mind at work, and he documents elements of it that boggle the imagination.

His survey includes cases in France, Russia, Poland, Italy, Spain, Portugal, Latin America, Belgium, the Netherlands, Germany, Scandinavia, the United States, and Great Britain. Although by now it might be difficult to obtain copies of this impressive great work, it more than succeeds in its stated goal. Absolutely one of the most fascinating reads ever!]

Dixon, Norman, PRECONSCIOUS PROCESSING, (John Wiley & Sons, New York, 1981). [Anyone interested in their own strange-mind faculties will ultimately have to accept two ascertainable facts – that they have strange-mind faculties, but also that there are difficulties with respect to becoming consciously aware of them. One reason for the difficulties is that information is processed preconsciously before it emerges into conscious awareness of it. Dixon reviews the converging lines of evidence for preconscious processing and perception without awareness, and preconscious determinants of conscious perceptual experience. It is meaningful to grasp how the mind is working beneath conscious awareness, so it is helpful to incorporate all of this into one's reality box. Although a bit challenging to read, his book includes numerous diagrams most of which are easy to understand.]

Inglis, Brian, NATURAL AND SUPERNATURAL, (Hodder and Stoughton, London, 1977). [Subtitled "A history of the paranormal," Inglis presents the first full survey of strange-mind phenomena from early times onward into the modern centuries. With scrupulous thoroughness and a wealth of detail, he draws on records of classical antiquity and on anthropological studies of primitive tribes. He pays particular attention to the work of the mesmerists and of the early psychical researchers in the last century.

Throughout, he relies on what peoples have actually

experienced, he avoids the trap of focusing on the problems of psychical and parapsychological research which largely ignore anecdotes of exceptional human experiencing at the individual level. In his mission to write this book, Inglis clearly approaches and broadens out a "bigger picture" of strange-mind experiencing. A "must" for any interested in their own strange-mind potentials.]

Inglis, Brian, TRANCE, (Grafton Books, London, 1989). [Subtitled "A natural history of altered states of mind," Inglis presents an intriguing and stimulating assessment of the evidence showing that many trance conditions seem to have served an evolutionary purpose. Trance hallucinations have acted as warnings or as sources of inspiration; hypnotism and hypnotherapy have proved effective in the relief of pain; hysterical laughter is a convulsive form of emotional relief; trance induction can remove the symptoms of some diseases. Trance has come to provide us with a link between our conscious selves and our subliminal minds, with their vast but only partially tapped resources. All "trance" or "altered states" of course reflect strange-mind activity."]

Schwartz, Berthold Eric, PARENT-CHILD TELEPATHY, (Garrett Publications, New York, 1971). [Subtitled "A study of the telepathy of everyday life," Schwartz, an M.D., and a psychiatrist, one of the few of that profession to undertake an in-depth examination of telepathy, inspired by witnessing it in his own children and in his practice. As many have realized through the ages, he confirmed that "Parents and children communicate in a variety of ways, and telepathy is one of them.

The telepathic way is the least known, but is the missing link, the new dimension in the fuller understanding of interpersonal communication." He examined the psychodynamics of telepathy; classroom telepathy in young children; classification of psychological and physiological hypotheses for telepathic episodes; the telepathic-hyperesthesia spectrum; tracer words and telepathy; telepathy and food; telepathic episodes and mental mechanisms; telepathy and motor behavior; built-in telepathic controls; and possible telepathic precognition. Many examples of child telepathy throughout. Sounds like a difficult read, but it isn't.]

Sinclair, Upton, MENTAL RADIO, (First published in 1930,

reprinted by Hampton Roads, Charlottesville, Va., 2001). [With a preface by Albert Einstein, this book reports on a lengthy and highly rewarding series of telepathic experiments the understanding of which is greatly enhanced by many drawings and sketches showing the accuracy and some pitfalls that emerge during the "mental radio" process. An absolutely fascinating read, and very well received throughout the world.]

Targ, Russell & Harold Puthoff, MIND-REACH, (Delacorte Press, New York, 1977). [Introduction by Margaret Mead, who indicates that the book "is a clear, straightforward account of a set of successful experiments that demonstrate the existence of 'remote-viewing,' a hitherto unvalidated [innate] human capacity." Presents the rationale and high points of the first seven years of government-funded remote viewing research at Stanford Research Institute (SRI) that began in 1972, and became world-famous thereafter. Many drawings and sketches achieved during experiments show various aspects of the strange mind at work.]

Warcollier, Rene, MIND TO MIND, (First published in 1948, reprinted by Hampton Roads, Charlottesville, Va., 2001, with a new preface by Ingo Swann.) [This is one of the most significant attempts to date to approach telepathy from the point of view of its own inner workings and processes. Two decades of experimentation are reported, and the author tells of how messages in the form of drawings were "sent" from one person to another, sometimes great distances apart, without known means of communication.

Details of imagery, imagination, language, and telepathic forms of communication illustrate many parallels between ordinary and strange-mind perception. A tentative theory of telepathy is presented in terms of association, motivation, and interpersonal relationships, and the dynamic mechanisms are described and made understandable.]

A BIOMIND SUPERPOWERS BOOK FROM
SWANN-RYDER PRODUCTIONS, LLC
www.ingoswann.com

OTHER BOOKS BY INGO SWANN

Everybody's Guide to Natural ESP
Master of Harmlessness
Penetration
Penetration: Special Edition Updated
Preserving the Psychic Child
Psychic Literacy
Psychic Sexuality
Purple Fables
Resurrecting the Mysterious
Secrets of Power, Volume 1
Secrets of Power, Volume 2
The Great Apparitions of Mary
The Windy Song
The Wisdom Category
Your Nostradamus Factor

Made in United States
Troutdale, OR
04/29/2024

19523959R00148